The Culture of Democracy

Cultural Sociology series

The Culture of Democracy

A Sociological Approach to Civil Society

Bin Xu

polity

First published in 2022 by Polity Press

Polity Press
111 River Street
Hoboken, NJ 07030, USA

Polity Press
111 River Street
Hoboken, NJ 07030, USA

ISBN-13: 978-1-5095-4398-4
ISBN-13: 978-1-5095-4399-1(pb)

A catalogue record for this book is available from the British Library.

Library of Congress Control Number: 2022930953

Typeset in 11 on 13pt Sabon
by Cheshire Typesetting Ltd, Cuddington, Cheshire
Printed and bound in the UK by TJ Books Limited

The publisher has used its best endeavors to ensure that the URLs for external websites referred to in this book are correct and active at the time of going to press. However, the publisher has no responsibility for the websites and can make no guarantee that a site will remain live or that the content is or will remain appropriate.

Every effort has been made to trace all copyright holders, but if any have been overlooked the publisher will be pleased to include any necessary credits in any subsequent reprint or edition.

For further information on Polity, visit our website:
politybooks.com

For Gary Alan Fine and Ming-Cheng Lo

Contents

Tables

Preface

The idea of writing this book came to me when I finished my first book, a cultural-sociological study of civic engagement under authoritarianism (*The Politics of Compassion: The Sichuan Earthquake and Civic Engagement in China*, Stanford University Press, 2017). I realized there was no book-length introduction that provided a road map of the cultural sociology of civil society. The absence of such a book is in stark contrast to the rapid growth of the field in the past three decades or so. The process of writing this book was concurrent with many challenges the world was facing, including the COVID-19 crisis, the protests in Hong Kong, the 2020 US presidential elections, and so forth. Hope emerged from upheavals like sunlight piercing through dark clouds, but the clouds have yet to dissipate. Meanwhile, many pressing concerns in today's world continue to worry us, such as the decay of civil life, polarization in the public sphere, moral-political dilemmas of humanitarianism, civil societies under authoritarianism, disinformation, climate change, and so on. I cannot say the cultural sociology of civil society has already offered ready-made answers for all these new and old issues. But at least this book is intended to confirm the merit of an art of listening. In a world where voices are too cacophonous and people are too busy to listen to each other, cultural sociology enables us to listen carefully to people's desires, imaginations, ideas, and stories, all of which cannot be reduced to organizations and political structures.

This book would not have been possible without the help I fortunately received. Special thanks go to two of my gurus, Gary Alan Fine and Ming-Cheng Lo, whose work on civil society, publics, and democracy has been a source of inspiration to me. Gary's idea of "tiny publics" is a significant part of my first book and this one. I also thank him for sharing his *The Hinge: Civil Society, Group Cultures, and the Power of Local Commitments* (2021) before it was published. Ming-Cheng's influence on my thoughts on civil society, especially in the context of East Asia, is so deep that only after I sent out a proposal to Polity did I realize that the title of this book bears such a close resemblance with that of her essay "Cultures of Democracy: A Civil-Society Approach"(2010) I thank Ming-Cheng for allowing me to infringe on her copyright, albeit unintentionally. To repay my intellectual debts, I dedicate this book to Gary and Ming-Cheng. I also would like to thank Jonathan Skerrett of Polity Press for being interested in this project and guiding me through the reviewing process, and Karina Jákupsdóttir for her help in the publishing process. I am grateful to the four anonymous reviewers for Polity for their helpful comments and suggestions. I particularly thank Kang Yi for reading the whole manuscript and providing valuable suggestions. Amin Ghaziani kindly shared his experience of writing his book in this "Cultural Sociology" series (*Sex Cultures*). I have also learned a great deal from my conversations about the topics covered in this book with friends and colleagues, including Deborah Davis, Nina Eliasoph, Yi Kang, Michael Kennedy, Shang Liu, David Palmer, Maria Repnikova, and Anthony Spires, among many others.

The final stage of writing and revising this book was supported by Emory University's Chronos Faculty Fellowship, which was generously provided by the Abraham J. & Phyllis Katz Foundation.

1

Introduction: The Culture of Democracy

> My family wrote a letter to me, citing the Bible (to encourage me), "I have fought a good fight. I have finished my course." Yet, the civil society I have endeavored to build in China is now on the edge of falling apart. And the universal suffrage I have been fighting for will not be achieved in Hong Kong any time soon. I have finished the course empty-handed. The only thing that gives me hope is that I have seen so many honest, kind-hearted faces along the way. (Chan 2020: 90)

Kin-man Chan wrote these words just before his release from prison in 2020. The term "civil society" summarizes his career and life. Chan, a Hong Kong-born, Yale-trained sociologist, spent much time promoting the idea and practices of "civil society" in Mainland China through his research, teaching, public speaking, and personnel training. He understood "civil society" not as a direct challenge to the authoritarian state but as a "parallel society," where citizens can organize their own public activities to improve the society. He aimed to build democracy from below, solidifying its social and cultural foundation before a representative democracy was possible. To do so, Chan even tried to seek the local Mainland government's cooperation and endorsement. This strategy put him in an awkward "middle-of-the-road" position. Oppositional activists in both the Mainland and Hong Kong criticized him for being too mild, and the Chinese government suspiciously watched his public engagement.

In 2013, Chan surprisingly announced that, along with two other activists, he was starting "Occupy Central with Love and Peace," a civil disobedience campaign initiative to advocate for genuine universal suffrage in Hong Kong. This initiative went beyond Chan's previous idea of a "parallel society"; instead, it directly challenged the Mainland authorities' intervention in Hong Kong. The campaign later became part of what was known as the Umbrella Movement in 2014. In 2019, a larger, more defiant anti-extradition movement, which will be detailed in chapter 5, broke out and then was brutally suppressed by the Hong Kong police. Chan found himself again in a dilemma. The younger, more militant activists challenged his belief in peaceful, reasonable, and nonviolent strategies, whereas the Hong Kong government viewed him as a main instigator of the movements. Consequently, Chan was arrested and sentenced to sixteen months in prison. The Mainland nongovernmental organizations (NGOs) associated with Chan were interrogated and raided. Meanwhile, the media and associational life in Hong Kong were forced into a corner. When I was completing this book in June 2021, *Apple Daily*, an influential newspaper famous for its criticisms of the Chinese government, was shut down. Hong Kongers flocked to newsstands to buy the last issue of the paper as a tribute to the demise of a once-independent and vibrant public sphere.

Outside Hong Kong, many people like Chan enthusiastically engage in associational life and speak in the public sphere. Not everyone is as prominent or as devoted as Chan, but some are. Most of the participants in civil societies are not jailed, but some are. Despite setbacks like that in Hong Kong, civil societies continue to exist and even thrive. The lasting vibrancy of civil society is remarkable against the dark backdrop of pressing problems in today's world, such as robust authoritarianism, polarized political debates, disinformation, widening socioeconomic inequality, and, most recently, rampant pandemic. During COVID-19, the United Nations Human Rights Council recognized the crucial role of civil society in responding to the pandemic, despite all the challenges civil society is facing: "civil society . . . is critical to providing accurate information about the situation and needs on the ground, designing responsive measures that are inclusive, safe and enabling, contributing to the implementation of measures adopted by the authorities, providing essential services and feedback on recovery and response measures, and pursuing transparency and accountability" (United Nations Human Rights Council 2021).

Part of the vibrancy of civil society comes from people's belief that they should and can solve many social problems through their public actions in accordance with their imaginations of a good society. They envision such a good society in various ways, not necessarily using the term "civil society." They also develop different norms and styles of their mutual interactions when they make concerted efforts to improve their societies. All these – the desire to build a good society, the imagining of such a good society, the understanding of their engagement, and the norm of their interaction – constitute the *cultural* aspect of civil society. Central to the cultural aspect of civil society is the *culture of democracy*, including cultural values, individual interpretations, and interaction norms about features of a democratic society, such as civility, independence, equality, liberty, tolerance, solidarity, inclusiveness, and so on (Lo 2010). The culture of democracy undergoes different interpretations and encounters various challenges. But it shapes people's actions, changes their lives, and alters political and social processes. It is real and significant.

In recent decades, sociologists have shown how a focus on the cultural aspect of civil society, particularly the culture of democracy, can help us understand some significant topics, including the public sphere, civil associations, individuals' civic engagement, global civil society, and civil societies in undemocratic contexts. This book introduces this booming scholarship, the *cultural sociology of civil society*, including its theoretical ideas, conceptual tools, and empirical studies. It tries to convince readers that cultural sociology represents an "art of listening" – a thoroughly empirical perspective that does not dismiss people's normative ideas about civil society, as some theories would do, but prioritizes a careful listening to the expressions of these ideas. This art of listening is what we need in this cacophonous world.

Let me first define several key concepts.

Civil Society

Much ink has been spilled over the concept of civil society. In its convoluted history, "civil society" has been used to refer to ideas as broad as society in general, including the market and even the state, and as narrow as only voluntary associations (Ehrenberg 2017). Without engaging in the conceptual debate, I define "civil society" by its four empirically identifiable components: civil society as the public sphere, as associations, as citizens' civic engagement, and as culture (Edwards 2020).

Civil society as the public sphere. The origin of the public sphere dates to ancient Athens, especially in *agoras* (public squares), where citizens met each other, traded goods, chatted, gossiped, and discussed public issues. Such public spaces for discussions also existed in other societies, such as the Middle East before modern times (Keane 2009: 123–53). But the concept of the "public sphere" did not become prominent in social sciences until Jürgen Habermas published his landmark book *The Structural Transformation of the Public Sphere: An Inquiry into a Category of Bourgeois Society*, in its original German version in 1962 and English translation in 1989 (Habermas 1989). Now, the term has a life of its own, has become one of those "celebrity" social science concepts whose stardom inevitably generates various interpretations and controversies. Here I use a *discursive* definition: the public sphere is a public space – institutional or physical or virtual – for *discourses*, that is, communication, discussion, and debate, about issues of public concern.

Civil society as associations. This might be the most common usage of the term "civil society," and thus, people often equate civil society with NGOs or "civil associations." In this sense, civil society includes various groups, associations, organizations, and their networks. They all share the common feature that they are relatively independent of states and markets, and the degree of their independence varies. Here's a list of typical examples: international NGOs like Médecins Sans Frontières (Doctors Without Borders) with chapters and member organizations around the world; smaller issue-based organizations like the Equal Justice Initiative, an American nonprofit organization founded by Bryan Stevenson to provide legal representation for wrongly convicted prisoners; parent teacher associations (PTAs) in local schools; professional associations like the International Sociological Association; feminist groups in China that fight against sexism in workplaces; a small group of volunteers who regularly work at a nursing home in Japan; and so on. The totality of associations is often called the "third sector" – as opposed to the state and the market – or the "nonprofit or voluntary sector."

Civil society as civic engagement. Neither civil associations nor the public sphere can exist without citizens' active participation in discussions of public affairs and their concerted effort to change society. Individual citizens are the foot soldiers of civil society. They are volunteers, NGO staff members, online users, residents who attend town hall meetings, and so on. Education institutions, governments, and organizations encourage civic engagement through informal practices and formal programs, such as the requirement for volunteering hours in high schools.

The term "civic engagement" usually includes two subcategories (Berger 2009): first, political engagement, which means activities related to political processes and institutions of states, such as voting, seeking or holding public office, writing letters to or calling representatives, lobbying, political campaigns, protests, circulating a political petition, and so on; second, social engagement, which means activities related to civil associations with goals to improve their society, including volunteering, fundraising, public discussions, and so on. This book mostly focuses on "social engagement" but does not overemphasize the distinction between "political" and "social" engagements because the two types of engagement are not always separable.

The Cultural Aspect of Civil Society

None of these three components – associations, the public sphere, and civic engagement – would constitute a civil society if they were not combined with the *cultural* aspect of civil society, the fourth component (Seligman 1995; Edwards 2020: 42–4). As John A. Hall describes, the concept of civil society is a "package deal," "being at one and the same time a social value and a set of social institutions" (Hall 1995: 2). This "package deal" observation rightly suggests that the cultural aspect is not a separate domain but an "aspect" of all other components "at one and the same time." Nevertheless, "culture" is more than "value." Contemporary cultural sociologists have developed at least four ways to define "culture" in civil society.

Culture in structure. In this definition, culture refers to the items in the "structure" or "classification" of symbols, meanings, moral principles, values, assumptions, and cognitive categories, which, in this case, pertain to what a good society should be. Culture in structure precedes and is independent of individuals. But it is neither monolithic nor static. Rather, it includes various items that are often in conflict with each other, and such items may change over time. Thus, it offers individuals multiple options of meanings to understand their social life, although in a certain social and historical context, the available options are limited. In the contemporary cultural sociology of civil society, two prominent theories represent this structural perspective. First, Jeffrey C. Alexander's *civil sphere theory* (CST) asserts that in a civil society there is an autonomous cultural structure of *binary codes*. Actors use such codes as a common language to communicate with each other, even if the contents of their views are dramatically different (Alexander 2006). Another structural theory is John W. Meyer's *world culture* or *world polity* theory. World culture includes rules, ethics, and norms about certain issues such as human rights and is formally defined in regulations, laws, and treaties at the global level (Lechner and Boli 2005; Meyer et al. 2009). International nongovernmental organizations (INGOs) are the major carriers of this world culture (Boli and Thomas 1997).

Culture in action. People may selectively draw upon some items but not others in the cultural structure they live under. They may also reinterpret the items to understand and justify their actions. Thus, cultural meanings are enacted in actions. This conception of culture in action highlights individuals' agency and the possibility of changes in structure (Swidler 1986; Sewell 1999). When used in research on civil society, its empirical focus is civil society actors' real-world actions to react to various situations, and their agency in picking and choosing different values about civil society in the cultural structure. For example, volunteers interpret their action as their contribution to society but may also use the language of expressive individualism ("volunteering makes *me* happy") to understand their actions (Wuthnow 1991). Organizations also strategically select values to define their goals and adapt to the cultural contexts they are working in (Swidler and Watkins 2017).

Culture in interaction. Culture also means norms of interactions, including conventions, rules, and expectations concerning appropriate ways in which individuals and groups engage in interactions in specific situations. Norms of interaction may or may not be the same as the values defined in the cultural structure because individual actors may selectively use and change the items in the structure to respond to the situations of their interactions. Norms of interaction also differ from cultures in action in that they are mostly the meaning-making processes *between* individuals rather than *of* individuals. In other words, from this perspective, the analytical unit is the interaction between at least two people, in a small group, and often at the meso level.

The concept of culture in interaction is deeply rooted in the rich tradition of microsociology (Goffman 1983; Fine 2012). It also dovetails with some of the most important theoretical ideas about civil society. The "civil" in "civil society" means not only values (culture in structure) and their interpretations (culture in action) but also civil norms of interactions among civically engaged citizens (culture in interaction) (Shils 1997). Some classical theories assert that all these three cultural dimensions should be consistent with each other. For Tocqueville, the civil norms of interactions are the "art of association," which citizens learn in their collective effort to address public issues and consolidate democracy (Tocqueville [1840] 2004). For Habermas, democracy hinges on the egalitarian, open, and rational norms of discussions in the public sphere (Habermas 1989). Contemporary cultural sociologists, however, reveal discrepancies among the three cultural dimensions. Civil associations must reconcile the need to address difficult public issues with the social desire to maintain order in interaction. Thus, they may mute discussions about public issues in their activities to avoid potential conflicts among their members (Eliasoph and Lichterman 2003). Pro-democracy associations may develop authoritarian norms of interactions among the members. Effective discussions in the public sphere may rely on emotions rather than Habermas's rational judgment (Bail et al. 2017). All these findings add complexities to the ideal situations in classical theories.

Culture in object. Culture also means *"cultural objects,"* which embody meanings in audible, visible, and tangible forms, such as movies, music, advertisements, novels, museums, and so on (Griswold 2013). Cultural objects go through the processes of production, dissemination, and reception and may change the meanings they originally carry (Peterson and Anand 2004). The cultural object approach is relatively underdeveloped in the cultural sociology of civil society, but the existing studies indicate strong potential for future research. For example, INGOs' design and dissemination of advertisements encounter difficulties and misuses in local contexts (McDonnell 2016). Images about human suffering in the non-Western context for humanitarian purposes ironically reify the spectatorship of Westerners and thus exacerbate global inequality (Chouliaraki 2013). Artistic and literary activities and projects are also common ways for citizens to be engaged in public affairs (Büyükokutan 2018).

It is worth noting that all these perspectives are only analytical distinctions. A social phenomenon can be examined from more than one of these perspectives, even in a single study. A study of volunteering, for instance, may focus on how individuals understand the meanings of their work (*culture in action*) and simultaneously on how they reconcile their own understandings with other volunteers' when they are working as a group (*culture in interaction*). Meanwhile, the prevalent ideas about volunteering in the broader cultural structure – compassion, individualism, altruism, and so on – shape their understanding and interactions (*culture in structure*). For this reason, a reader may find a study discussed in more than one chapter of this book.

The Culture of Democracy

The most prevalent and influential culture in today's civil societies is the *culture of democracy*.

To define "culture of democracy," we first need to define "democracy," another essential but complex concept (Held 2006; Keane 2009). In this book, I follow John Dewey's definition: democracy is "more than a form of government" – an electoral system of representation, the rule of law, and the checks and balances among the legislature, the executive branch, and the justice system. Rather, it is also "primarily a mode of associational living, of conjoint communicated experience" (Dewey 1916: 87). Along this line of thinking, some theorists argue that civil society and state institutions are two necessary components of a democracy (Keane 1998: 7–8) and that civil society is one of the necessary conditions for a consolidated democracy (Linz and Stepan 1996). This idea is consistent with the underlying assumption of some democratic theories that challenge the dominant *representative liberalism*, which is centered on a competitive election system. For example, *the participatory liberal theory* stresses ordinary citizens' direct participation in decision-making processes in their communities. *The discursive theory*, represented by Habermas and other theorists, asserts that inclusiveness should be achieved through open, civil, egalitarian, reasonable deliberation. *The constructionist theory* highlights popular inclusiveness but argues that some socially constructed categories, concepts, and norms may limit powerless people's participation (Ferree et al. 2002a). In short, "democracy" in the "culture of democracy" means *democratic social life*.

Then, what does *culture* in "culture of democracy" mean? For cultural sociology, as discussed above, the "culture" in the "culture of democracy" refers to at least three interrelated dimensions. First, as *culture in structure*, it refers to values about the

9

features of a democratic society. Second, such values inform people's imagining of a democratic society but must be enacted in public actions which aim to pursue and maintain a democratic social life. Thus, it is *culture in action*. Third, it is a democratic *norm of interaction* among engaged citizens, such as equal, open, tolerant, nonviolent, and inclusive manners of communication and styles of self-governing. All three aspects of the culture of democracy exist in real civil societies, in real people's minds and actions.

In sum, the *culture of democracy* refers to values about democratic social life, people's imagining of a democratic society, and democratic norms of their interactions, all of which are involved and realized in their concerted effort to build a democratic society.

The culture of democracy is central to the culture aspect of civil society. This statement is not theorists' arbitrary judgment. Rather, it is an observation that the culture of democracy historically originated from at least three major transformations in the second part of the twentieth century. The term "civil society" emerged from these historical transformations as an idea *of* and *for* democracy.

First, "civil society" was believed to be incarnated in the development of independent social spaces under Communism in Central and Eastern Europe in the 1960s–1980s (Kennedy 2002), as well as the "Third Wave Democracy" in Southern Europe, Latin America, sub-Saharan Africa, and Asia-Pacific. These processes inspired people to link civil societies to the potential of democracy under undemocratic regimes, although such linkage remains open to debate.

Second, some scholars and public figures in Europe and the United States were worried about the health of their established democracies. Symptoms, as they believe, included the decline of "civil society" – more specifically, the decline of "social capital" – and rampant individualism (Putnam 2000; Bellah et al. 2008 [1985]). In the United States, America as a nation of "joiners" and American democracy based on a moral community – a mythical image derived from the very beginning of the country – were believed to be in a crisis, and the solution was to reinvigorate the civil society. In the United Kingdom, a similar solution was proposed by politicians and intellectuals, such as David Blunkett, who advocated for the renewal of democracy through rebuilding a strong civil society and civic culture.

Third, the acceleration of globalization has weakened nation-states' role in regulating citizens' social life and strengthened transnational, global associations and the public spheres, especially after the end of the Cold War (Kaldor 2003). Correspondingly, universal values and ideas about human rights, equality, and so on have been realized and diffused in the global practices of international organizations, activists, and participants of public discussions (Meyer et al. 1997; Lechner and Boli 2005). On the other hand, such diffusion intensified the debate over democracy – mostly, Western democracy – and whether and how it is inter-woven with imperialism and neoliberalism.

A product of these entwined historical changes, the culture of democracy is not a homogeneous, static set of values but full of dynamics, contradictions, and conflicts. The culture of democracy exists in the cultural structure of civil society, but its items may be in constant conflict with each other. People also often selec-tively use these items in their discourses and actions: for instance, emphasizing "liberty" but downplaying "equality." The same cultural term in the democratic cultural structure also can be used to express various ideas that range from the right to the left on the political spectrum. For example, "liberty" can mean an antago-nism toward the state or the emancipation of underprivileged groups from the dominance of the market. A democratic norm of interaction, for example, solidarity and equality, may be practiced in the internal interactions among members of a group but not extended to outsiders whose social characteristics are different from theirs. Organizations and individuals following the culture of democracy can be simultaneously inclusive and exclusive, solidary and repressive. A certain association emphasizes their "civil" char-acters but meanwhile paints a negative picture of other "uncivil" groups, and such characterization may justify their exclusion-ary practices and rhetoric (Alexander 2006). Others may have a publicly stated goal to pursue some aspects of a democratic social life, but their internal interactions may follow norms quite differ-ent from or even opposite to the culture of democracy: exclusive membership, hierarchical relations, and explicit racism. Moreover, many associations and civil society actors do not pursue democracy. All these complexities result from the fact that the culture of democracy exists at the intersections of social fault lines, such as class, ethnicity, gender, regions, nation-states, and so on.

Nevertheless, cultural sociology observes that, while various other cultures exist in civil societies around the world, the culture of democracy remains the most influential, even though such influence is most visible when the culture of democracy is contested, challenged, or altered. Many cultures of civil society are different renditions of the culture of democracy. They may mix key elements of the culture of democracy with other cultural items, some of which are even antidemocratic. Others develop their own nondemocratic cultures as responses to the global diffusion of the culture of democracy. The challenges, however, signify the centrality of the culture of democracy.

Why Cultural Sociology?

Cultural sociology is an empirically grounded perspective that focuses on the cultural aspect of civil society, especially the culture of democracy. Thus, it differs from other common perspectives by offering distinctive answers to two key questions: First, does culture matter in civil society? Second, is the culture of democracy the only culture or the only legitimate culture in civil society? (See table 1.1.)

The "normative perspective" gives "yes" as answer to both questions. It asserts that culture matters greatly in civil society and that the culture of democracy is – and should be – the only or the only legitimate culture in civil society. From this perspective, civil society and the culture of democracy are both normative concepts. This perspective is prevalent in political theories and corresponding ideas that guide real-world civil society practices, for example, NGOs' statements and advertisements, in which "civil society" is often equated with an ideal society with equality, openness, and democracy. These features are used as a benchmark to judge real-

Table 1.1 Different perspectives on civil society

	Normative perspective	Cultural sociology	Minimal-culture perspective
Does culture matter in civil society?	Yes	Yes, but "culture" means many things	No
Is the culture of democracy the only or the only legitimate culture in civil society?	Yes	No, but the culture of democracy is central	No

world civil societies; some are qualified, bona fide civil societies, whereas others are not. Such a perspective is not wrong within the boundary of political theory. But when it is used in social scientific research it provokes controversies.

Even in the heyday of this normative perspective, the 1990s, when the fall of Communism was celebrated as a triumph of civil societies in Central and Eastern Europe, scholars cautioned against the tendency to idealize civil society and mix the normative with the analytical. Sociologist Krishan Kumar expresses this caution: "'Civil society' sounds good; it has a good feel to it; it has the look of a fine old wine, full of depth and complexity." Nonetheless, Kumar continues, "fine old wines can stimulate but they can also make you drunk" (Kumar 1993: 376). Charles Tilly also claims that the concepts of civil society and the public sphere are "morally admirable but analytically useless" (cited in Emirbayer and Sheller 1999: 145). For many social scientists, "civil society" seems to be little more than "chicken soup for the social scientific soul." Its normatively heartening implications become its analytical liability. Other critics, in a more poignant way, point out that the normative perspective has the political overtone that the liberal democratic culture originated from the West is the gold standard for the rest of the world.

To remedy this issue, social scientists develop a "minimal-culture perspective" on civil society. It answers "no" to both questions: culture does not matter much in civil society, and the culture of democracy certainly is not and should not be the only game in town. Its solution is simple: excising the cultural aspect, adopting a bare-bones analytical concept, and reducing "civil society" to organizations and actors who are engaged in realpolitik or provide social services. In this way, this perspective believes, the normative trouble of "civil society" can be shaken off, and the concept can be refurbished into a purely analytical one.

The cultural sociology of civil society shares with both perspectives some common ground but also differs from them on some significant issues. Like the normative perspective, it gives the answer "yes" to the first question ("Does culture matter in civil society?") and thus eschews the minimal-culture perspective's dismissal of culture. Nevertheless, the cultural sociology of civil society offers a much broader, more empirical definition of "culture," including not only "culture" as "values" in the normative perspective, a typical culture-in-structure concept, but also culture in action, culture as norms of interaction, and culture in objects.

Cultural sociology answers "no" to the second question ("Is the culture of democracy the only culture or only legitimate culture in civil society?") and, in this sense, leans toward the empirical approach of the minimal-culture perspective. Yet, unlike the minimal-culture perspective, cultural sociology emphasizes that although the culture of democracy is not the only culture of civil society, it is still the most significant. It would be erroneous to deny the fact that the culture of democracy inspires and encourages numerous people to participate in various public activities to improve their societies and build a democratic social life.

In sum, the cultural sociology of civil society is a thoroughly empirical perspective that takes the cultural aspect of civil society seriously. Cultural sociologists do not use the culture of democracy as a normative standard to judge real-world civil societies; rather, they recognize the fact that it is the central, most influential culture in the past and current historical contexts of civil society. Cultural sociologists study the culture of democracy empirically. Neglecting this cultural aspect of civil society does not make an analysis more objective. Instead, it makes such an analysis incomplete.

This Book

The Culture of Democracy: A Sociological Approach to Civil Society is an up-to-date, comprehensive introduction to the cultural sociology of civil society, which, for the first time, pulls together various strands of this booming scholarship into a single volume. It takes a global perspective. It devotes about half of its space to discussions of civil societies in the non-Western regions, including Asia, Latin America, Africa, and the Middle East. It also presents global and transnational associations and public spheres that transcend national borders.

The following chapters are arranged in a logical order. Chapters 2–4 cover the cultural aspect of three main components of civil society: the public sphere, associations, and civic engagement. Chapter 5 examines how the culture of democracy historically emerged in undemocratic contexts and how it is still entangled with undemocratic states and changes of democratic cultures in those contexts. Chapter 6 broadens the scope from the territories of nation-states to global civil society, including INGOs, citizens' volunteering in other countries, and discourses in transnational public spheres. The concluding chapter briefly recapitulates the main points in previous chapters and emphasizes the merit of cultural sociology as an art of listening amid the cacophonous voices in today's civil societies.

A few words are in order here to clarify the goal and scope of this book. First, this book is not an introduction to the whole field of civil society; rather, it surveys a particular approach, that is, the cultural sociology of civil society, and how this approach sheds light on some important issues in academic research as well as real-world civil societies. Second, while this book mostly draws on sociological studies, it often ventures out of disciplinary boundaries to include theories and studies in other fields, such as political science, media studies, political theory, and anthropology. Cross-fertilization is a merit instead of a weakness, and there is no need for intellectual patrolling along artificial disciplinary borders. Finally, I deliberately leave some related subfields and topics – such as social movements and the media, two important parts of civil society – to other, more specialized books. The reason for this omission is more practical than theoretical: these topics are already established subfields in their own right; introductory texts to them are widely available (Jasper 2014).

2

Values, Codes, and Styles in the Public Sphere

Jürgen Habermas's concept of the "public sphere" remains one of the most significant yet controversial concepts in modern social science (Habermas 1989). To understand the concept and its controversy, you can try picturing Habermas's favorite epitome of the bourgeois public sphere, a coffeehouse. On a cold, misty day in London, as the stereotype of eighteenth-century England goes, a patron entered the coffeehouse, hung his (yes, more likely a man than a woman) coat on a peg, and started to talk with other men. The coat would have told us about this person's social identity: the equivalent now would be a businessman's nice suit, or an ordinary office worker's plain jacket. But with all coats hung on pegs, the wearers' identities were suspended and bracketed. The topics of conversation were important public issues, and the conversations were egalitarian, inclusive, and rational: no shouting matches; no curse words; and even when debates occurred, all engaged parties expressed their opinions in a respectful manner. To Habermas, this was what the culture of democracy looked like.

This is just a myth, you might say. Yes, the reality is messier. Scholars, including Habermas himself, have shown that such an ideal has never been fully realized. Various social identities – race, nationality, class, gender, and so on – and their corresponding inequalities are rarely suspended or bracketed in public discussions. Even when identities appear to be suspended, that is probably because people with certain identities are already excluded from the public sphere. Access to public spheres, from

17

the coffeehouse to the Internet, is often unequally distributed. Women were excluded from most public spheres in eighteenth-century Europe. In most societies today, one must have a certain level of income to pay for newspapers, the Internet, transportation, and so on, to enter public discussions. Even coffee is unequal: 25 *yuan* a cup in a Starbucks in China is not an insignificant amount for many Chinese with monthly incomes between 3,000 and 5,000 *yuan*. Moreover, as we all know too well, mediated discourses are not always rational. We have witnessed in recent years ubiquitous disinformation, "alternative facts," and even outright lies, not just from ordinary people but from people with tremendous power and influence.

Despite all these challenges, Habermas's classical theory of the public sphere has inspired numerous studies and theories, including some significant theoretical breakthroughs in the cultural sociology of civil society. "Culture" here mainly means two things: moral-political *values* and *codes* in the cultural structure, and *norms* and *styles* of discourses as a type of social interactions. In Habermas's classical treatise, civility, reason, openness, and equality are not only values democratic citizens should adhere to but also norms of their conversation. Cultural sociologists, however, use their empirical studies to show how such ideals are always intertwined with complexity in real-world discourses.

Three Types of Discourses in the Public Sphere

In this book, the public sphere is defined as a discursive space where the main actions are discourses. But what kinds of discourses are there? (See table 2.1.)

The first type of discourse is *local conversation*, informal discussion about public issues among people who gather in local, small public spaces, such as coffeehouses, salons, bookstores, and restaurants. In those settings, citizens feel more comfortable, less nervous when they are talking. Local conversations usually do not lead to binding decisions; they are conversations for conversations' sake. Serious discussions about public issues are often

Table 2.1 Three types of discourses of the public sphere

	Definition	Setting	Examples
Local conversation	Informal, local conversations about public issues	Small groups, local meeting places	Discussions in coffeehouses and salons Underground bookstores in Eastern Europe under Communism Breakfast conversations in a local corner store in Michigan
Mediated discourse	Discussions, opinions, and debates in mediated spaces	The media and the Internet	Live debates on TV Op-eds Letters to editors Online discussions
Formal deliberation	Discussions and dialogs governed by explicit rules	Formal programs organized by governments or civil associations	Town meetings in America Participatory budgeting assemblies in Brazil *Gram sabha* (village assembly) in India

interrupted by gossip, jokes, and small talk. But local conversations are important because they are the most everyday form of discourse in the public sphere.

The second type, probably the most common connotation of the "public sphere," is *mediated discourse* – opinions, discussions, and debates about public issues that take place in mediated communicative spaces, such as the mass media and the Internet. Most of us encounter mediated discourses on a daily basis and sometimes join them: debates among TV commentators, opinions expressed through op-eds, discussions in online forums, posts and interactions on social media, and letters to editors.

The third type is *formal deliberation*, including discussions and dialogs among citizens about public issues in formal programs organized and managed by governments and civil associations. Formal deliberation differs from the other two types of discourses in its clearly defined and implemented goals, procedures, and rules. Typical cases of formal deliberation include the famous "town meetings" in New England in the United States, in which local citizens meet to discuss and make decisions on public issues about their communities (Bryan 2004). Contemporary formal deliberation flourishes in non-Western contexts, such as Brazil's "participatory budgeting" meetings (Baiocchi 2005) and India's *gram sabha* (village assembly) (Rao and Sanyal 2010). Numerous experiments and practices in those deliberation programs constitute a significant movement of *deliberative democracy* around the world (Gutmann and Thompson 2004).

All these types certainly are just analytical distinctions; in real-world public spheres, the boundaries are less clear-cut. A self-organized civic group may start with discussions in a local café, but gradually become an active participant in a government-sponsored dialog program and regularly speak to the media about certain public issues. Many civic groups which regularly meet in person are also based on social media, where members seek each other out and attempt to influence public opinions.

Jürgen Habermas: The Public Sphere as a Realm for the Culture of Democracy

Habermas's concept of the *public sphere* contains two dimensions of the culture of democracy: the democratic *values* of openness and equality, and the critical-rational and egalitarian *norms* of interactions (Habermas 1989). The two dimensions ideally should be one and the same. What citizens gain from discourses in the public sphere is the ability to communicate with each other in a free, rational way, which helps emancipate people from the power of the market and the state. Thus, the public sphere can provide a social-cultural foundation for a democratic society.

For Habermas, the ideal public sphere has never been fulfilled in history, but the "bourgeois public sphere" in seventeenth- and eighteenth-century Europe in places like coffeehouses and salons was probably the closest to the ideal. The bourgeois public sphere originated in a gradual separation from the private sphere (family, for example), the state, and the market. Such separation happened in the High Middle Ages, accelerated in the seventeenth century, and matured in the eighteenth century. A few historical processes were the driving forces of this separation, including the development of a market economy and corresponding demands for information, the growing public relevance of private families, the formation of nation-states, and the emergence of the press.

At the heart of the bourgeois public sphere was what Habermas terms "critical-rational debates," in which people used reason to discuss public issues and question other people's opinions. Such critical-rational debates, Habermas argues, suspended social status as well as the laws of the market and the state, at least temporarily. Such suspension or bracketing of external social status, as Habermas cautiously points out, was within certain limits – participants being mostly educated people, bourgeoisie who owned properties, and nearly always men.

With the development of the public sphere, this type of local conversation turned into mediated discourses. The states gradually engaged themselves in the struggles with the public sphere as the public opinion made its way to parliament at the end of the eighteenth century. The functions of the public sphere were also spelled out in the law, including a set of basic rights that concerned the public's engagement in rational-critical debates, such as freedom of opinion and speech, freedom of the press, freedom of assembly and association, and so on.

Local Conversations

Many scholars, however, have pointed out that Habermas's view of local conversations is too romantic (Calhoun 1992). The simple fact, as Michael Schudson (Schudson 1997) points out, is that conversations are just conversations. The pleasure of being together and talking in a sociable manner is the most common norm of local conversations. There is nothing democratic in conversations per se; nor do local, face-to-face conversations, however serious, always help democratic values and institutions.

Even when local conversations revolve around serious political issues, scholars argue, Habermas underestimates the possibility that other identities and cultures infiltrate conversation (Calhoun 1992). For Habermas, the state and the market take the blame for the distortion in communications, but the larger society – with its diversity and inequality – seems to be shut out of the café. In critiquing Habermas's argument, Nancy Fraser rightly contends that bracketing social inequality often works to the advantage of dominant groups in society and to the disadvantage of subordinates (Fraser 1992). Well-dressed gentlemen in a coffeehouse spoke to the fewer working-class guests "as if" they were equals – that is, without talking about why there were so few less-well-dressed folks in the discussions. Fraser contends (1992: 120, italics added): "This conception [bracketing inequality] assumes that a public sphere is or can be a space of *zero degree culture*, so utterly bereft of any specific ethos as to accommodate with perfect neutrality and equal ease interventions expressive of any and every *cultural ethos*." This important critique paves the way for many studies of how "cultural ethos" – various kinds of identities and corresponding cultural values and styles of conversation – other than the rational, open, and equal culture in Habermas's original theory also are expressed in local conversations.

For example, Katherine Cramer Walsh studies a group of white, middle-class, mostly male retirees who regularly met for morning coffees and random chats at a "corner store" in Ann Arbor, Michigan, where the University of Michigan is located (Walsh 2004). Their morning coffee conversations were "a good way to start off the day" but often involved comments on local and national politics – at the time of the research, the Clinton–Lewinsky scandal, for example. Instead of engaging in an open, rational-critical discourse, the members of the corner-store group patrolled the boundaries of their self-proclaimed identity as "hard-working middle-class folks with moderate values." As one of the members said, "What you get in there is the common touch. None of that philosophy and theorizing [points toward the university], and they aren't destitute poor people who do a lot of bitching. Just common people, middle people" (2004: 44). Outsiders, especially

Black Americans, women, and young people, who also frequented the store, were unable or unwilling to join their conversations. This identity boundary was also physical: the group occupied two large tables in the middle of the corner store, while others often sat at small tables in the other corner. No one crossed this boundary.

Walsh's later book in 2016 extends and develops the identity-based argument to explain low-income Wisconsin residents' surprising support of Republican Governor Scott Walker, whose policies and political orientations tend to increase income disparity, undermine labor rights, and hurt low-income voters. To explain why those residents voted against their own interests, Walsh (Cramer) joined informal group discussions in various places. She found that rural residents of Wisconsin who regularly participate in those discussions had a clear-cut identity based on the place they lived, that is, "rural consciousness." This rural consciousness contained three general elements: "(1) a belief that rural areas are ignored by decision makers, including policy makers, (2) a perception that rural areas do not get their fair share of resources, and (3) a sense that rural folks have fundamentally distinct values and lifestyles, which are misunderstood and disrespected by city folks" (Cramer 2016: 12). Scott Walker and the conservatives, rather than the "urban" educated folks, were believed to be those who cared about rural identities. In conventional wisdom, "rural identity" is more often linked to developing countries where there are greater rural/urban divides. Yet Walsh's study shows that such identity also exists in developed countries like the US. Her study, published in 2016, also provided insights for understanding the power of the rural/urban divide in subsequent events, such as the US presidential elections in 2016 and 2020 and COVID-19 vaccination hesitancy.

In Habermas's theory, the informality of local conversations is a strength because it can accommodate those who flinch from formal discourse. But Walsh's and other studies show its downside. Informal local conversations could be cases of "birds of a feather flocking together": members share common demographics and identity, and their regular interactions strengthen their group identity and lead to more rigid symbolic and political boundaries.

What we see in those studies are small, self-serving islands isolated from each other in a sea of civil society. This image may not be surprising to readers of this book because groups talking past each other rather than across social divides has been a phenomenon more visible than ever in the polarizing public spheres around the world.

Some researchers use the focus group method to lend formality to local conversations to see if things would be different. This idea is not just a methodological change but of theoretical and political significance. It tests representative liberalism, the dominant theory of democracy. Representative liberalism doubts ordinary people's ability to acquire information and understand complex ideas. It then proposes a division of political labor: average folks elect their representatives and do not have to worry about their participation, especially given that everyone is busy on other issues; the elected politicians and elites do the deliberation. Now, scholars ask: what if the "average folks" are given chances to deliberate and talk in settings with slightly more formality? Their conversations in those settings are still largely casual, informal, but they are given issues, topics, and some rules of conversation. This kind of focus group discussion resembles formal deliberation but does not exactly replicate it.

These researchers' findings challenge the condescending views of representative liberalism. Ordinary, working people, they found, can construct meanings in their discussions of complex issues, critically use media discourses, and make coherent arguments, despite some apparent obstacles, such as lack of political experience, education, and time. William A. Gamson's study pioneered this approach (Gamson 1992). In the 1980s, Gamson and his assistants recruited thirty-eight groups with 188 participants from Boston areas to learn how they talked about four given issues that were significant at the time: affirmative action in employment, nuclear power safety, troubled automobile and steel industries, and the Arab–Israeli conflict. For each group, a trained facilitator stated the issues, asked open-ended questions, used political cartoons as vignettes, and navigated the conversations without controlling the conversation flow. The overall atmosphere of the conversations was more casual than formal: people were asked to recruit their friends; the conversations took place in living rooms; refreshments were provided.

The researchers found that the participants used various sources according to different issues: personal experience (stories about "my co-workers" or "my friend's friend") was used much more often in discussions of affirmative action than in discussions of other topics. Moreover, a set of clearly defined values and counter-values – or, in Gamson's terms, "themes" and "counterthemes" – could be found in varying forms in discussions of different topics. Themes are taken-for-granted assumptions approved by the main-stream culture, and counterthemes challenge those assumptions. For example, when discussing the "troubled industry" scenario, that is, the collapsing automobile and steel companies receiving bailouts and handouts from government, most participants clearly used the countertheme of "popular democracy." They invoked the popular wisdom that the rich managed to get richer no matter what, with another mainstream cultural item, "self-reliance," to embarrass the enterprises getting government handouts. These counterthemes, however, were not prominent in the media dis-courses. Even when the same theme was used, different groups framed their discussions in different ways. For example, the "self-reliance" theme of the discussions of affirmative action contained different meanings in groups with different racial configurations. Black groups pointed out the disadvantage for ethnic minorities if a color-blind policy was implemented, whereas the white and interracial groups tended to think of equal opportunity for all individuals as a universal standard regardless of race (Gamson 1992: 135–51).

Gamson's study provides a more optimistic image of "average folks" than Walsh's Ann Arbor and Wisconsin groups. An expla-nation of this difference might be the setting of local conversation: in the focus group setting, participants might appear guarded and care more about what they say and how they appear to others, whereas the natural setting might unleash some thoughts and expressions which the participants would not voice in a more formal way.

Nancy Fraser's other important criticism of Habermas is that his theory assumes a single, overarching public sphere. In various contexts, however, there are always many *counter-publics* such as nationalist publics, peasants' publics, women's publics, working-class publics, and so forth, which contest the exclusionary practices of the bourgeois publics (Fraser 1992: 116). Pretending not to see these counter-publics is like dancing to the tune of the powerful: the less powerful are culturally incorporated into a false "we." "The ideal of participatory parity," Fraser argues, "is better achieved by a multiplicity of publics than by a single public" (1992: 127).

Counter-publics exist everywhere (Warner 2002), but perhaps the best cases are under repressive regimes, for example, in Communist-era Central and Eastern Europe, underground bookstores, private gatherings, intellectuals' salons, and avant-garde theaters. In those publics, the communication modes distanced themselves from and often challenged the coercive, dominant political cultures. People met and performed the "normal" functions (attending friends' social gatherings, buying books, rehearsing and watching plays, and so on) but, more importantly, talked with each other about political issues and developed the capacity for political actions. The interactions in the counter-publics followed some implicit norms. For example, Jeffrey Goldfarb describes the interactions in an underground bookstore (Goldfarb 2006: 11):

> One approached it with first a brief telephone call and then a ring on the doorbell. The door opened. Polite regards from a mutual friend were exchanged, followed by a query concerning the latest number of an underground publication. It was available and produced for the customer. The price was stated, then paid. The buyer and seller acted like buyer and seller. They were not oppositionist heroes. This was the everyday life of the opposition, which included a nice profit for "bookstores," and for publishers and writers.

Everyday but hardly trivial, the bookstores sold banned books by "dangerous" intellectuals in the Soviet bloc, such as Sakharov, Solzhenitsyn, Brodsky, Havel, Michnik, and Kuroń. What is theoretically interesting about these counter-publics is the discrepancy between their culture as values and their culture as norms of interactions. Their values obviously included ideas related to the pursuit of democracy under authoritarianism, but their conversation styles were far from open: rather, they talked to each other in a clandestine, exclusive way, due to political repression. The two cultures, however, combined to generate a force that played an important role in the civil societies in Central and Eastern Europe (chapter 5).

Under contemporary authoritarian regimes, such small counter-publics also exist widely, but not necessarily in defiance of the regimes. For example, Yemenis gather in public places to chew *qāt* (khat) (leaves of an Arabian shrub, which socially function as an equivalent to coffee as a stimulant for conversation), and to discuss various issues ranging from marriage arrangement to politics (Wedeen 2008: 120–47). These gatherings manage to survive in the crevices of the political system. The Yemeni regime certainly puts restrictions on the *qāt* chews but sometimes tolerates their existence because they serve as a window onto the society, and the regime can keep tabs on potential challengers of the regime.

The *qāt* chews vary in size, openness, and topics. Some are open to anyone who wants to take part, revolve around political topics, and thus serve as the counter-publics for citizens under the authoritarian regime to have local conversations. Participants often bring their own *qāt*, and thus the organizers do not have extra financial burdens. Some *qāt* chews are more formal, especially those gatherings where politicians of the oppositional parties meet with their would-be constituencies. Such formal *qāt* chews have rules to regulate conversation, tend to have long speeches, and sometimes end before everyone has a chance to speak. Consequently, more *qāt* chews are held as "follow-up" sessions; or people may write letters to weigh in to express their opinions. Informal *qāt* chews are more unstructured: a gathering event may cover multiple topics, and participants talk in a more spontaneous way without intervention from the host. The topics in both formal and informal chews could be politically subversive: for example, journalists share their experience of being harassed and persecuted. But some could be abstract and theoretical, such as meanings of national identity, that is, Yemeni-ness. The openness of the *qāt* chews is in sharp contrast to the dire straits of Yemeni politics: violence, rigged elections, and political suppression. The existence of such publics does not mean that they will necessarily influence policymaking, though sometimes they do. Rather, "creative forms of contestation are deliberated in *qāt* chews, which are part of a mediated process of producing public awareness in various parts of the country" (Wedeen 2008: 131). Internally, the *qāt* chews are not free from social fault lines: the gatherings are segregated by gender – women tend to organize and attend those with small topics, whereas men dominate the political ones; the seating at the gatherings is usually arranged by social ranks and status. Overall, the norms of interactions in those counter-publics are a mixture of equal, open conversations and stratified, restricted communications.

Formal Deliberation

If the informal, local discussions are perfectly rational-critical debates and not interrupted by banter and gossip, then can they be directly translated into a democratic discourse? Michael Schudson gives a negative answer (Schudson 1997). He argues that what distinguishes democratic conversations from those everyday conversations is that democratic conversations are intended to solve problems, governed by rules, and composed of participants with various backgrounds.

Formal deliberation is a mechanism for such democratic conversations. Formal deliberation is at the heart of the theory and practice of *deliberative democracy*, a form of democratic governance in which "free and equal citizens (and their representatives) justify decisions in a process in which they give one another reasons that are mutually acceptable and generally accessible, with the aim of reaching conclusions that are binding in the present on all citizens but open to challenge in the future" (Gutmann and Thompson 2004: 7).

Deliberative democracy has four features, which are consistent with the ideal culture of democracy implied in the concept of the public sphere: reason-giving discussions, discussions accessible to all citizens, with a binding decision as the goal, and a continuing dialog. Deliberative democracy is proposed to remedy problems of *aggregate democracy* based on the majority rule. Aggregate democracy downplays the importance of discussions and, thus, accepts and even reinforces the existing distribution of power. Deliberative democracy theorists argue that if there is no available mechanism for everyone to discuss the options to vote on, then voting alone would hardly be justified as a healthy democracy. Deliberative democracy proposes that everyone sit down, collectively learn about their options, give reasons in their discussions, and, after all these are done, reach a decision or start a vote. This theory has been tested and developed in various practical innovations in civil society, such as deliberative opinion polls and various public dialog programs (Gutmann and Thompson 2004; Fishkin 2009).

Many deliberation practices emerged in the New Left movement and Third Wave Democracy, in non-Western contexts, where local practices have affinity with the culture of democracy. An important case is India's *gram sabha*, which works like a legislature at the village level to elect the *gram panchayat* (village council), the governing institution of a village. A *gram sabha* meets twice a year, and every villager who registers on the election roll has the right to be a member of the *sabha*.

The tradition of *sabha* dates back to Buddhism, Jainism, and Hinduism in as early as the fifth century BC. The word *sabha* (assembly) originally indicated a meeting in which various opinions and ideas are debated without being dominated by caste elders. This tradition showed its affinity with the Western democratic culture when Henry Maine, a British legal expert who was appointed to advise the Indian government in the 1860s, articulated a theory of village self-government. Maine's theory influenced the British colonial government, which passed an Act in 1920 to set up the first formal, democratically elected village councils. His theory also influenced Mohandas Gandhi, who made self-governing villages the emblem of a "perfect" democracy based on the principles of nonviolence, decentralization, and cooperation. In the current Constitution of India, article 243A grants *gram sabhas* the status of "village legislature." They are particularly successful in the progressive state of Kerala, where the participation of lower-caste groups and women has significantly improved, although poverty, caste, and gender disparity still hinder the functioning of this deliberative system (Parthasarathy and Rao 2018).

Similarly, the "participatory budgeting" meetings in Porto Alegre in Brazil serve as a form of public participation in decision-making processes and public discussions (Baiocchi 2003). At first glance, the districts where the participatory budgeting program was carried out could not be more different from the ideal public sphere: low education level, low incomes, slums, crimes, and poor infrastructures. More broadly, the Brazilian political culture "emphasizes private entitlement and privilege over the public good and the rights" (Baiocchi 2003: 56), the opposite of the cultural expectation for civic participation. Yet a large-scale experiment of "participatory budgeting" was built on this flimsy foundation and yielded astonishing successes.

The original purpose of the participatory budgeting meetings was for ordinary citizens to discuss and decide on government budgets. But citizens also used the meetings to express their opinions and engage in deliberation about other issues. The participants in the assemblies often interrupted the agenda by sharing local news, discussing social problems, and even calling for demonstrations. Conflicts occurred in the form of shouting matches and even almost exchanging blows. The issues that triggered the conflicts included public and personal problems. Part of the reason for the regular conflicts unrelated to the agenda was that the assembly meetings were the *only* public sphere in the community for local activists and participants to air their grievances and discuss public problems.

The cases of *gram sabha*s and Porto Alegre participatory budgeting provide several interesting points for thinking about the culture of democracy. First, formal deliberation can develop in a political-cultural context where the culture of democracy is mostly imported and often entangled with complex local traditions. Second, effective public deliberation programs often rely on the state's involvement instead of being completely grassroots. Leaders, ruling parties, and democratic institutions play a decisive role. For example, in Porto Alegre, the local government, which then was controlled by the progressive Workers' Party, actively adopted the institution of participatory budgeting. India's institution of *gram sabha*s was a result of political leaders' philosophy of democracy, which was later incarnated in laws. Third, in Porto Alegre's case, the discourse-oriented public sphere emerged from the budgeting assembly meetings, a problem-solving occasion, and, in this sense, it reveals the unmet demands for public forums at the local level. All these common features show that the culture of democracy in formal deliberation in non-Western contexts is a result of joint forces of institutions, ideas, and practices.

Styles and Norms of Discourses in Formal Deliberation

The formality in formal deliberation, however, does not guarantee a style or norm of discourse that fits well with the rational-critical debate presumed by the classical theory of the public sphere. It encounters similar problems to those in local conversations, and participants sometimes improvise to conduct conversations in ways unanticipated by the classical theory.

Storytelling. Classical theorists of the public sphere often dismiss storytelling. Stories use emotions rather than reasons; they may be partial, biased, unrepresentative. Good stories might be too good because they may attract disproportionate attention toward those who can tell touching, sensible stories rather than those whose ideas are great but whose stories are less impressive.

In actual practices of deliberation, however, storytelling is ubiquitous. A disbeliever can just go to any town hall meeting or other formal deliberation occasions to count the number of personal stories. Moreover, while the criticisms of storytelling are well taken, sociologists find that stories can also help achieve the goal of an open, inclusive public discussion. For example, personal stories can be an equalizing mechanism which encourages disadvantaged groups to share their otherwise marginalized experience. Personal stories can help people overcome lack of knowledge on highly specialized, technical issues because telling a story may make them feel less "stupid" and more authentic in front of others (Ryfe 2006: 78). In critical race theory, "counter-storytelling" is regarded as a theoretical, pedagogical, and methodological tool to challenge racism, sexism, and classism (Solórzano and Yosso 2002).

Storytelling in public deliberation is not limited to marginalized groups. People use stories in public debates to explore and justify their views. In this sense, abstract reasoning and storytelling are not separated but melded together. The stories people tell in formal deliberation are also not limited to personal stories but include historical events, current affairs, and even popular culture, such as the movie *Gattaca*, which is used to talk about the practice of screening human embryos before implanting one in a woman's uterus (Edgell et al. 2016).

Sociologists Francesca Polletta and John Lee investigated twelve formal groups of 263 people who deliberated online about how to rebuild the World Trade Center site in the wake of the 9/11 attacks (Polletta and Lee 2006). They show that stories perform independent functions for public deliberation instead of relying on normative principles to be effective. But the functions of stories are shaped by the issues, contexts, and other factors related to the debates. For example, personal stories illustrate a point or a practical idea or imaginatively flesh out the implications of a position. Personal stories also help define a new set of issues as worthy of discussion. Such stories resort to personal experience to establish the storytellers' authenticity and authority: "I have experienced that, and therefore my opinions are worth listening to." On the other hand, telling personal stories appears less often in deliberation about policy-related, technical issues.

A key finding of these researchers' study is that, in contrast to the ideal-type, unambiguous reasoning in public debates, personal stories' capacity sometimes comes from their ambiguity. Stories sometimes do not present explicit morals and thus encourage tellers and listeners to collaborate in a dialog to figure out the "morals" and other possibilities through further discussions. This openness to interpretation facilitates disadvantaged groups' participation.

Adversary and solidarity. No public sphere can be free from conflicts. How do people engaged in public deliberation and discussion deal with the inevitable conflicts, meanwhile maintaining solidarity among themselves? This balance between adversary and solidarity is also deeply rooted in relations between two notions of democracy. One is *adversary democracy*, which asserts that people's interests are in constant conflict and that conflict will lead to adversary deliberation (Mansbridge 1983). The only solution, then, is to vote. A healthy and effective democracy, according to this notion, is not meant to eliminate conflict but to make sure that everyone's interests are accurately represented.

But voting can lead to what Tocqueville calls "the tyranny of the majority": voting losers' interests are not reflected in the final policy decision, especially when the margin in the voting outcome is tiny. If 50.1 percent of a town with 1,000 people vote to cut property taxes or not to pave a road, then 499 residents of the town will suffer from fewer school buses or may have to walk on a muddy road every day. The majority vote "no" simply because they have no schoolkids or because they drive to work, but the 499 people's grievances remain unresolved. Thus, voting is not a solution to the division and conflicting interests. Rather, it leads to more divisions.

In contrast, the *unitary democracy* theory starts from the assumption that people often share common interests. For members of a small community, such common interests are obvious and undeniable: safety, water quality, reliable infrastructure, and other public goods. The members also know each other, have repeated face-to-face interactions, and enjoy at least a minimum level of solidarity with each other. No one wants to get a dirty look at a local restaurant because he or she provokes a debate at a town meeting. This natural aversion to conflict often gives rise to a different kind of democratic process: sitting down to deliberate about options, understanding each other's point, showing mutual respect, making decisions based on consensus rather than voting, and, afterwards, remaining good friends and nice neighbors.

One might think of this unitary democracy as too utopian. Yet, as Mansbridge argues, it is actually the oldest form of collective problem solving (Mansbridge 1983). In a hunter-gatherer society, consensus often formed through discussions in a small human group with common interests. Athenian democracy was a combination of unitary and adversary democracies in a city-state. Even in a complex society with more sophisticated division of labor and social inequality, unitary democracy remains important, especially in smaller social units. Any reader who is an American professor can recall how many times the faculty of your department reach a positive consensus on a junior professor's tenure decision. In fact, most decisions are consensual, and the reason is simple: it is hard to deny granting tenure to someone who has already had six years of face-to-face interaction with everyone in the department, even if this person may have slightly below-average performance. In comparison, deciding on hiring is often split, and such a split is expected: it does not cost much if you eliminate someone whom you've only met briefly during a campus visit, even though this candidate may have stronger credentials than some existing faculty members.

The problem, however, is more empirical than normative: how do the unitary discourses interact with the adversary ones? In most local public spheres, Mansbridge argues, unitary and adversary democratic discussions exist at the same time and often shift back and forth. Unitary discourses tend to achieve consensus when there are common interests; but in most cases, interests are both common and conflicting, and therefore, unitary discourses often fail to protect the disadvantaged.

Mansbridge demonstrates this point in a fine-grained study of town meetings in the small town of "Selby" (a pseudonym) in Vermont, a classic form of formal deliberation in a classic place since New England town meetings had become an emblem and myth for American democratic social life. "Selby" was a poor town with only about 350 adult citizens, including "old-timers" – farmers who had lived in the town for a long time – plus new-comers, working-class and middle-class people who moved to town, the rich and the poor. Their apparently conflicting interests were reflected in the debates at the town meetings. Debates revolved around various issues, such as zoning, which may benefit rich investors more than poor farmers.

The sense of community and belief in their common interests ("We are all friends") set limit to the debates, however. The residents dreaded conflicts, quarrels, public speaking, and looking foolish, and thus they tended to avoid town meetings. Out of the same fear of conflicts, the selectman (elected town official) and government directors informally negotiated with each other about candidates and policy options before the meeting. But these practices also blinded people to the conflicts, made them believe that the decision-makers would make the best decisions for them, and eventually left them confused and helpless.

In other cases of formal deliberation, the tension between solidarity and adversary also exists between participants of deliberation and those professional organizers and practitioners. As organizing and moderating formal deliberation becomes a small industry, practitioners share a relatively stable set of ideas about what the "public" is and what kinds of deliberation and dialog are effective. They formulate the ideas into guidelines in their handbooks or training manuals. For example, the practitioners emphasize that participants in public deliberation should speak as "I" instead of "we" – in other words, not as representatives of a group but as individuals (Polletta 2020: 96). "Speaking for yourself," the practitioners believe, will move people away from their original preference and change their ideas in the process of dialog. This willingness to change is the essence of deliberation, they hold. Moreover, the practitioners hope that the "I's" will turn into a renewed "we" based on the bonds created in the discussions, becoming friends across social divides. The ways of creating such bonds go beyond Habermas's classical view of "reason-giving." Rather, trading jokes, telling stories, and being passionate are all fine. This "we," however, should not be a new political identity based on advocacy. The purpose is to get ordinary people's voices heard.

Participants, however, often have different understandings of what they are doing in deliberation (Polletta 2020). They start with a sense of "we" in addition to "I." For example, in two series of forums in New York City that Polletta studied, the participants claimed that their forums were "a microcosm of New York" and that they "represent[ed] a voice of the city," and even compared the forums to the United Nations, in which each of them "represented" a part of the city. Many participants also wanted to see their recommendations have specific impacts on decision-making in the government. But the deliberation professionals highlighted the necessity for "having ordinary people's voice heard" and emphasized their neutrality on the issue of pressing the government to adopt the recommendations from deliberation. They tended to develop a relationship of "power with" instead of "power over" the authorities (Polletta 2020: 107–8). The cost of this strategy, however, was to disappoint the participants who wanted to push for real changes through the deliberation.

Identity and inequality. To form an inclusive public sphere, many formal deliberation programs are designed to talk *about* and talk *over* identity differences based on race, class, and gender. But questions remain: Will such an emphasis on identities lead to division among the participants and breakdown of the deliberation? On the other hand, if unity is highlighted and identities are downplayed, will the discussion become mere tokenism and even facilitate and reproduce existing power relations?

To answer these questions, Katherine Cramer Walsh studied voluntary groups involved in a civic dialog program about race, a sensitive topic in the United States, and found that the deliberation conveyed a great deal of ambivalence about the proper balance of unity and diversity (Walsh 2007). Many groups started their deliberation with a strong stance privileging unity – "We are all the human race" or "People are people" – or simply questioning the necessity of addressing difference and diversity. Yet racial and ethnic differences quickly emerged and then dominated the discussions. Sometimes the discussions revolved around proper racial and ethnic labels ("Latino" or "Hispanic" or "Chicano") and took the form of information gathering and clarification. But such exchanges sometimes went further and became an open debate over whether racial labels are necessary at all. A white participant questioned whether racial labels mattered since "We are American," whereas others insisted that labels mattered: for example, "Blacks" or "African Americans" were OK labels for them, but the term "colored" only brought back the traumatic history of slavery and violence. When a white participant denied the need to pay attention to racial difference, those Black participants who previously agreed on unity began to disagree. The white participant also back-pedaled and admitted that as a white he did not have the experience to notice the importance of difference.

This pattern of push and pull over the tension between unity and difference repeatedly occurred in many conversations. When one person, usually white, sounded a theme of unity, people of color clearly urged the group to pay attention to racial difference and even discrimination. "In other words, a white person might say, 'I had no idea that my African-American neighbor is followed through the store every time she shops for food.' And an African American might say, 'I had no idea that whites had no idea!'" (Walsh 2007: 115).

In the end of the sessions, most participants reported that their "eyes had been opened" (2007: 114). A cynic might suspect that such conversations may just skim the surface and even border on playing tokenism. Yet what was remarkable was that the participants themselves knew their effort could be interpreted in that way. They used action – striking up a friendship by inviting a participant of a different race to have a drink for the first time – to demonstrate they wanted to know more about each other.

Class identity also shapes the discursive style of formal deliberation. In India, the *gram sabhas*' main goal is to select beneficiaries of government resources and allocate public goods (Rao and Sanyal 2010). In this highly hierarchical and plural society divided by caste, ethnicity, and wealth, the *gram sabhas* give the poor and lower-caste members an opportunity to air their grievances and challenge the prevailing inequalities. Rao and Sanyal believe that the *gram sabhas* were like a "sacred sphere" in Emile Durkheim's sense: a sphere in which core values of equality and inclusiveness were celebrated through passionate engagement or "collective effervescence."

Nevertheless, inequality remains in this "sacred sphere" and shapes how people talk. Individuals from the disadvantaged groups momentarily discard the stigma attached to their identities and make their otherwise "hidden transcripts" visible. Higher-caste villagers, in contrast, tend to avoid the *gram sabha*, dismissing it as a government-imposed affirmative action to benefit lower-caste villagers. When they do participate, they tend to adopt an aggressive discursive style to assert their primacy over other claims. For example, a high-caste member says that their demand for cemented roads must be met: "We don't care in the least about other development activities. First of all, we need cement roads. That's it" (Rao and Sanyal 2010: 160). Lower-caste villagers, in contrast, tend to be less aggressive and stress that their demands and even occasional aggressive manners are not a sign of disrespect. What complicates this caste distinction is the economic class distinction. Higher-caste but poor individuals challenge the fairness of the affirmative action based on caste by claiming that they, despite their higher caste status, are left behind by the redistributive policies.

Formal deliberation is also gendered. Women participants of the public sphere are implicitly or explicitly discouraged from expressing their ideas and engaging in more serious talks. When they actually engage, they talk for less time, and their opinions are more likely to be dismissed as trivial (Conover et al. 2002). Though women make up more than half of attendees of *gram sabhas*, they tend to have less floor time, are less likely to initiate conversations, are often ignored by male participants, and are less likely to get a response from government officials. The following deliberation in a *gram sabha* is a typical example (topics in bold) (Parthasarathy et al. 2019: 625):

Female 1: There are many wells in our village, but **the wells are without a pulley wheel**. Moreover, since the water is not used for any purpose, it gets wasted. So if you can **de-silt the wells**, we can not only use the water for drinking purposes but for other purposes also . . .
Male 1: The kitchen has been constructed in the balwadi [pre-school]

in our village. It is not used. Please arrange for the **construction of a toilet for women**. We also need a play ground for games. The canals are muddy. We have to **de-silt the canals. We need a library** . . .
Male (Official): We have a library in our panchayat. We have arranged for five magazines – an English paper, The Hindu, and four Tamil magazines. All the elderly persons and children are reading. I am also asking the officers **to improve the library and have passed a resolution** in this regard. We have already **de-silted the canal** and cleaned it under Mahatma Gandhi Rural Employment guarantee scheme.

Two issues "Female 1" raised were ignored, and she was interrupted by "Male 1," who raised three different issues. While Male 1 might sound "nice" to women when he advocated for a toilet for women, his interruption demonstrated the power difference in the discursive style. The male official only responded to Male 1's issues and completely ignored Female 1's requests.

Would a female leader or facilitator of deliberation change the gendered discursive style? The findings are mixed. Ramya Parthasarathy, Vijayendra Rao, and Nethra Palaniswamy find that the presence of a female president does not affect the likelihood of female citizens participating in *gram sabhas*, but the participating women are more likely to set the agenda for the deliberation under a female president (Parthasarathy et al. 2019: 637). Polletta and Chen confirm the positive impacts of the presence of women facilitators and managers for American programs of deliberation. But they argue that such impacts depend on the gendered institutional setting or field for the deliberation (Polletta and Chen 2013). If a field is masculinized, for example, explicitly or implicitly setting norms according to men's preference and rewarding masculine actions like making statements and engaging in conflicts, then gender inequality prevails. If a field is feminized, that is, encourages feminine actions like expressing emotions and empathetic listening, then access to the deliberation and the talk between men and women tend to be more equal.

In their study of "Listening to the City," a citizens' forum on rebuilding the 9/11 site, Polletta and Chen found no evidence of gender inequalities in the discussion. Women posted as many messages as men; women were as likely as men to advance opinions. Gender differences certainly existed but did not translate into gender inequalities. For example, women were more likely than men to use personal stories to back up their opinions, but they were no less likely to express their opinions directly. The reason for this gender equality was that the contemporary field of organized public deliberation had become "feminized," which meant "the field has developed in a way that has valorized stereotypically female modes of talk" (Polletta and Chen 2013: 304). Although the field of public deliberation in the United States was championed mostly by men, the idea of "deliberation" was realized in "dialogs," which emphasized empathetic listening, expressing emotions, and building community. This union of dialog and deliberation was particularly suited for women to get involved and play a significant role. Certainly, this involvement was facilitated by a gender stereotype that women are better at those tasks, but this stereotype positively enabled women to get advanced degrees or certificates to become most of the local organizers and facilitators.

Even so, scholars warn that the presence of female organizers and leaders is "no panacea for the deeper problem of women's general silence" (Parthasarathy et al. 2019: 638). That women feel comfortable with a female organizer already speaks volumes for the intrinsic gender inequality in deliberation. In contrast, mansplainers need no such encouragement to entitle themselves to set the agenda.

Values and Codes of Mediated Discourses: The Civil Sphere Theory

Mediated discourses, the discourses in the mass media and on the Internet, are probably the area where most cultural sociological work concentrates. Some significant theoretical and methodological advances have occurred in this area in recent decades. Among them, as outlined above, Jeffrey C. Alexander's civil sphere theory (hereafter CST) (Alexander 2006) is one of the most important. In this theory, civil society is conceptualized as a *civil sphere*, a sphere defined by a set of universal *binary codes* that serve as a common language for various participants to understand and talk about what is civil and democratic and what is not. The civil sphere is crystallized in and sustained by "communicative institutions," such as mass media, public opinions, and polls, and "regulative institutions," including voting, political parties, offices, and laws. The civil sphere constantly interacts with the non-civil spheres, such as the state.

At the heart of the civil sphere is *solidarity*. The idea of solidarity can date back to classical sociology, especially Durkheim's distinction between *mechanical solidarity* (solidarity among members of a homogeneous society, who share the same beliefs and values) and *organic solidarity* (solidarity among functionally differential people who do not share the same values). When the division of labor in a society becomes more complex, Durkheim argues, organic solidarity dominates. You and your banker share the organic solidarity based on the functions your banker performs and, at a deeper level, on your self-interests, instead of mutual affection and common belief (Durkheim 1933).

Do people in a large, modern, and complex society need common feeling, value, and belief in addition to their need for each other's services and goods? This is a fundamental question for modern sociology, which cannot be discussed in full here. Suffice to say that Durkheim himself, especially in his works on religion and morals, highlighted humans' need for symbols, rituals, and religions to develop mutual feelings and form the common belief that a society as a whole is higher than individuals (Durkheim [1912] 1995).

These kinds of common feelings and beliefs are where Alexander and other modern Durkheimian scholars start to develop their theories. Alexander asserts (Alexander 2006: 3):

> societies are not governed by power alone and are not fueled only by the pursuit of self-interest. Feelings for others matter, and they are structured by the boundaries of solidarity. How solidarity is structured, how far it extends, what it's composed of – these are critical issues for every social order, and especially for orders that aim at the good life.

Table 2.2 The binary codes in CST

	Civil	Anti-civil
Motives	Active	Passive
	Autonomous	Dependent
	Rational	Irrational
	Reasonable	Hysterical
	Calm	Excitable
	Self-controlled	Wild-passionate
	Realistic	Distorted
	Sane	Mad
Relationships	Open	Secretive
	Trusting	Suspicious
	Critical	Deferential
	Honorable	Self-interested
	Altruistic	Greedy
	Truthful	Deceitful
	Straightforward	Calculating
	Deliberative	Conspiratorial
	Friendly	Antagonistic
Institutions	Rule-regulated	Arbitrary
	Law	Power
	Equality	Hierarchy
	Inclusive	Exclusive
	Impersonal	Personal
	Contracts	Bonds of loyalty
	Groups	Factions
	Office	Personality

Note: This table is a compilation of the binary structures presented in Alexander (2006: 57–9).

A cynic might demur: do people really have a common belief? This suspicion makes sense, particularly against the backdrop of the disenchantment of modern society, the decline of religions, the rise of multiculturalism, and so on. But Alexander's theory of civil sphere avoids the theoretical pitfall that common beliefs mean the same set of faiths, doctrines, and ethics. Rather, he argues that common beliefs are stated in the same set of *binary codes*, which define what a good society is. (See table 2.2.) The "good" or "pure" side of the binary codes constitutes what people believe a good society should look like, even if the usage and interpretation of the codes vary. For example, people should be reasonable, autonomous, and self-controlled; they should form relationships that are open, friendly, and truthful; and civil institutions should be equal, inclusive, and rule-regulated. The opposite are the "polluted" codes, which constitute the characteristics of anti-civil people, relationships, and institutions.

The binary codes represent a typical concept of "culture in structure." Those who find binary codes baffling can think of the codes as *langue* (an abstract language system such as English, including its grammar and vocabulary) and the actual mediated discourses as *parole* (or speech). Although actual speeches may express conflicting ideas, people still speak the same language, use the same vocabulary, and follow the same grammatical rules.

Let's do a quick exercise by using a recent example (italics added to highlight the codes). In the aftermath of the American presidential election in 2020, Trump supporters accused the Democrats of stealing the election, using several negative codes in table 2.2 to describe the Democrats as *deceitful, conspiratorial* "deep state" political forces using *calculating* tricks and their *power* to violate *laws*. The Democrats – and some Republicans – also used codes in the same binary system, even the same codes, to condemn the accusation as a groundless "*conspiracy* theory" used by the Trump administration to mobilize *wild-passionate* and even *mad* supporters to sabotage the democratic electoral system and *laws*. No one in the debate used the negative side of the codes to describe themselves; everyone believed they were defending American democracy. Despite their polarized "*parole*," they spoke the same "*langue*."

Binary codes are universal rather than particularistic. People who may not share the same specific faiths or ideas often share the same "language" to talk about a good society and democracy. Everyone wants to be on the side of rational, altruistic, and law-abiding, but what exactly those words mean could be dramatically different to different people.

This leads to a crucial but often misunderstood idea in the CST: there is always a tension between universal codes and particularistic ideas. Alexander accepts this tension as part of the dynamics of the civil sphere and makes two further arguments. First, it is exactly this tension that compels the civil sphere to evolve, mostly in the process of debating over how and why the society still has not realized the universal values in real-world practices and what should be done. Second, despite the tension, people still share the same codes, and this commonality suggests the possibility of communication and interaction across the political divides. The common codes thus are the basis of civil solidarity. The divided house still stands on the foundation of the universal language of democracy, although the house is constantly shaking.

Alexander, however, gives an important warning: the binary codes could be solidary and repressive at the same time. Each pair of codes is binary, defined by its contrast to its opposite: what is rational is defined by its contrast to the irrational. When people apply positive codes to certain groups, often themselves, as law-obeying and honorable people, they simultaneously apply the negative sides of the codes – unlawful, greedy, and so on – to others. Thus, stigmatized groups will be marginalized or even expelled from the civil sphere.

Alexander argues that this paradox – commitment to civil codes coexisting with exclusionary practices – is an intrinsic feature of the civil sphere. This argument distinguishes the CST from utopian concepts like Habermas's public sphere. Instead of defining a social space as ideal and the rest as the dark side, Alexander asserts that the dark side is just the flip side of the bright. Both sides constitute the binary codes. Neither can exist without the other. The non-civil spheres, such as states, families, economy, and so on, do not "colonize" the civil sphere. Rather, the civil sphere is always nested in the non-civil spheres through processes of compromise and fragmentation (2006: 195).

This subtle theory may sound complex, but human history is littered with familiar examples of this paradox. In numerous cases of ethnic and racial discrimination, the core ethnic groups of the civil sphere ensconce themselves on the positive side of the civil codes – for example, highlighting their civil nature, such as being educated, civilized, rational, and decent – but depict marginal groups as the opposite. Their claims about their civil nature might be just hypocritical. In many cases, however, they *may* have all these self-proclaimed features, and their commitment to core values like liberty *may* be sincere. But their civility and sincerity do not exist without defining the marginal groups as their opposite; such negative definitions are sometimes materialized in brutal exclusions and even killings.

So, is there any hope for a democratic civil society to get better since the tension is intrinsic and can never be eliminated? Yes. But, unlike many normative theories that place their hope on a particular realm, or class, or idea, the CST suggests that hope and despair are two sides of the same coin, and contradictions are the driving force of progress. The negative side of the civil sphere creates its own counterforce, *civil repair*, a cultural and institutional process in which the marginalized, allegedly "uncivil" groups may resort to the core values of the civil sphere (such as equality and inclusiveness) to demand to be included in that sphere, in other words, to "repair" the damages caused by exclusion and repression. To do such civil repair, the marginal groups must distance themselves from their particularistic positions and interests and persuasively communicate a broader vision of the problems to the society at large. In other words, they need to anchor their claims in the universal promises of the collective good in the civil sphere, that is, using the positive side of the binary codes (justice, equality, and so on) instead of the negative side (self-interests). In sum, the shared codes in the culture of democracy make people recognize the imperfection and limitation of the actual civil sphere and, thus, provide them with a language to repair the civil sphere. Modern civil society, therefore, is a never-ending process of civil repair.

Applications of the Civil Sphere Theory

The best cases for the CST include two kinds. First are the mediated discourses with divided opinions but the same democratic codes. For example, in an early study, Alexander and Smith analyze the public debates over the Iran–Contra crisis in the 1980s (Alexander and Smith 1993): the Reagan administration sold arms to Iran, which was subject to an arms embargo, in return for Iran using its influence to release American hostages held by Islamic groups, and then used the money from the arms sales to support the "Contra" guerrillas in Nicaragua. In a congressional hearing on this matter, the representatives who denounced the Reagan administration used the negative codes to describe the Iran deal as something "secretive" concealed by "lies," concluding, therefore, that such a "conspirator" government should not be trusted. Lieutenant-Colonel Oliver North, the infamous officer directly involved in the affair, defended the administration by using the positive side of the codes. He argued that his problematic methods to deal with Iran were used to pursue goals with a higher good, for example, to release American hostages, to gain autonomy in making decisions about the Middle East, and to support the guerrillas to end the tyranny of the Communist regime and give liberty to the people of Nicaragua. He also put himself on the positive side: he claimed he had no motives other than pursuing patriotic and democratic causes.

The second type of best cases for the CST include those with both exclusion and inclusion of marginal groups and corresponding "civil repair" in the expansion of the civil sphere. Alexander reinterprets the classic case of the American Civil Rights movement as a success in translating the particularities of African American demands into the universal idioms and institutions of the American civil sphere (Alexander 2006). Alexander argues that, despite their disparity in the hierarchical social order, Black and some white Americans shared the same civil sphere, which was based on the same codes of liberty, such as justice, tolerance, equality, and so on. These codes were mostly sustained by the Northern communicative and regulatory institutions, which invaded the Southern non-civil spheres, especially local governments. The communicative institutions and the Black leaders created well-known dramas, such as the Montgomery bus boycott, to provoke violent repression; played out themes in the innermost structure of the American civil sphere, such as nonviolence, justice, and equality; and gained sympathy from the Northerners.

While the American Civil Rights movement is a triumphant story for the civil sphere, the Jewish incorporation into the European civil sphere ended with horrendous atrocities (Alexander 2006). Western Europe had a developed civil sphere in the nineteenth and twentieth centuries, where modern democratic values of liberty, equality, and solidarity originated and prevailed. The values – or democratic codes – were real, cherished by most people rather than fabricated or only instrumentally used. And these values, together with the communicative and regulative institutions, had the tendency to expand universal claims about equality and civility to even subordinated out-groups.

This expansion of the civil sphere, however, had its repressive side. It "assimilated" out-groups into the civil sphere by "purifying" their "uncivil" qualities, in Jews' case, mostly related to their religion. In other words, if assimilation was to "free their universal personhood from the polluted qualities attached to it, members of Jewish communities would have to learn either to repress or eliminate their Jewishness" (Alexander 2006: 466). The Jews as an out-group were confronted with a dilemma: individual persons could be assimilated into public life, but the qualities related to their religion remained despised. The pressure from the core group led to some self-changes in reinterpreting and distancing from Jewish religious ideas, but such self-changes provoked backlash movements, which eventually led to the Orthodox and Conservative denominations. But overall, the Jews' asymmetrical assimilation, which was somewhat successful, in no way mitigated the stigmatization of their religion's qualities (2006: 483). This dilemma intensified in the second part of the nineteenth century, and the failure to change themselves led to Zionism, an effort to physically withdraw from Western civil societies. Yet this withdrawal was not a solution to the Jewish question. The "final solution" came in a bloody form: the Holocaust. In the United States, such an assimilation failure was avoided only because of World War II, when the Nazis were defined by the negative side of the democratic codes and Jews gained a better status in the democratic culture, although the asymmetric assimilation never disappeared.

The Civil Spheres in Non-Western Societies

Two questions that naturally emerge when CST evolves: "Can CST realize its generalizing ambition through application to empirical realities beyond the American and Western contexts? Can it shed light on the dynamics of societies with very different histories and cultural values and traditions?" (Palmer and Alexander 2019: 1). In recent years, Alexander has collaborated with scholars around the world and produced edited volumes and journal articles to answer these questions (Alexander and Tognato 2018; Alexander et al. 2019; Alexander et al. 2020; Alexander et al. 2021), and other scholars inspired by the CST have also tested and expanded the theory in non-Euro-American societies (Lo and Fan 2010).

A major finding in this scholarship is what Ming-Cheng Lo and Yun Fan term *hybrid codes*: the underlying political cultural structures of many non-Western civil spheres contain more sets of codes than Alexander's original binary codes (Lo and Fan 2010). These codes derived from the legacies of dictatorship, authoritarianism, colonialism, and various other moral and religious cultures. Moreover, facing those potentially contradictory codes, marginal groups not only seek incorporation into the existing civil sphere – the goal highlighted in Alexander's theory – but also attempt to change the dominant codes.

This idea was illustrated in a series of studies of East Asian societies. In a comparative study of political cultures in Taiwan and Hong Kong, Ming-Cheng Lo and Christopher P. Bettinger conducted inductive coding of political cartoons and found that two sorts of codes – codes of caring and codes of bureaucratic efficiency, in addition to the original democratic codes laid out in Alexander's theory – were also significant in the mediated discourses. The patterns of combination of those codes varied in Taiwan and Hong Kong (Lo and Bettinger 2009). In a study of women's images in political cartoons, Lo and Fan found that female characters, such as nurses and TV anchorwomen, use the code of caring – compassion, reciprocity, and interdependence – to provide evaluations of the quality of discourses and solutions to the problems (Lo and Fan 2010). Thus, they are more rational, compassionate, and reasonable than hysterical men.

Underneath these non-Western codes is a challenge to the mainstream, Western-centered narrative that East Asian values – often viewed as relational and sentimental as opposed to individual and rational – are incompatible with the culture of democracy. For example, in popular perceptions and academic discourses in the Chinese-speaking world, *guanxi* (personal connection) is often accused of being a particularistic ethical norm that justifies noninstitutional, informal, often corrupted connections. Therefore, it is believed to be incompatible with the modern market economy and the rule of law. In a theoretical article, Lo and Eileen Otis challenge this idea. They argue that *guanxi* can be used by civil society actors to understand and help their engagement, for example, using familial language like "sisters" to unite women to pursue their labor rights and using hometowns as ties to form associations among migrants (Lo and Otis 2003).

Hybrid codes exist in other parts of the world. For example, Gianpaolo Baiocchi shows that in Brazil there is a "corporate code," which emphasizes the importance of hierarchical relations and a person's ties to a collectivity and powerful people instead of individuals' rights and independence. The corporate code "represents the cultural residue of the powerful interests of ruling landed elites and a powerful state" (Baiocchi 2006: 287). This code is often interwoven with the liberal democracy codes. The temporal dimension of the civil sphere codes in Brazil is also important: the increasing use of the liberal code is concurrent with the democratization process. In Baiocchi's study, the corporate code dominated the 1979–82 public debate over prison reforms before democratization. The corporate code gives rights to only those who work. Therefore, prisoners, who were "privileged" to be idling, had no rights. If rights were given to those idling prisoners, as some arguments went, it would threaten the well-being of the society. The arguments for criminals' human rights, however, also sometimes drew on the corporate code, for example, idleness versus work, but in a different way: horrible conditions need reform because prisoners are idling and "graduate from the school of crime –

the prison – and are thrown back into society" (*Jornal do Brasil* 25 May 1979, quoted in Baiocchi 2006: 298).

In contrast, the 1992 debate over impeaching President Fernando Collor de Mello, the first democratically elected president since the dictatorship, was framed much more in the liberal code than the corporate code (Baiocchi 2006). While the argument against him highlighted the corrupt president as a threat to democracy, the argument for him emphasized he was democratically elected by 35 million Brazilians and had accomplished many things, including a series of modernizing reforms. Using the liberal codes, President Collor accused those who intended to impeach him of attempting an antidemocratic coup. In some situations, the corporate code was also used to defend the president: for example, he was depicted as a representative of the poor, the majority of the working class, and the protector of the people against the wealthy and the privileged. The underlying corporate code of this rhetoric is a combination of populism and paternalism: connecting the powerless mass – rather than individuals – to the powerful protector, who fought against the privileged elite on their behalf.

Similarly, as Botello and Magnoni show, the Mexican civil sphere is dominated by not only the democratic code but also the "patrimonial code," which allows political leaders to use patrimonial power in authoritarian ways without many legal consequences. This patrimonial code, however, also requires the leaders to know the limit of their power and practice it in a restrained way (Botello and Magnoni 2018). This hybrid was evident in the public debates over the "white house scandal": President Enrique Peña Nieto and his wife acquired a luxury white house from a company which had won important infrastructure projects from Peña Nieto's administrations since he was the governor of the State of Mexico. Investigative journalists and public opinion depicted the presidential couple as representations of the polluted side of the democratic codes. Some criticisms were also derived from the patrimonial code, accusing the president of violating the traditional norm of self-restraints. Most of those who relied on the patrimonial code, however, tended to defend the president and condemned the critics for their self-interested accusation. The collective response in the civil sphere finally forced the president to support institutional reforms to regulate conflicts of interest. As in Brazil's case, the temporal dimension is worth particular attention: patrimonialism was a legacy of the pre-democratization regime in Mexico and still plays an important role in the civil sphere.

Styles and Norms of Mediated Discourses: Civility, Emotion, and Drama

Much theoretical discussion of styles of mediated discourses revolves around *civility*. Civility as etiquette exists in any historical period and any society. But mere etiquette may belie social inequality. Aristocrats' emphasis on proper decorum functions as a mechanism to exclude lower-class people. Democratic civility, instead, is rooted in the notion of individuals' equal rights to participate in open mediated discourses; such discourses should be conducted in a reasonable and respectful manner not for manners' sake but out of genuine respect for everyone's rights and opinions. Edward Shils articulates this idea (Shils 1997: 338):

> Civility as a feature of civil society considers others as fellow-citizens of equal dignity in their rights and obligations as members of civil society; it means regarding other persons, including one's adversaries, as members of the same inclusive collectivity, i.e., as members of the same society, even though they belong to different parties or to different religious communities or to different ethnic groups.

There is no single criterion of democratic civility. Different cultures of democracy emphasize different aspects. In their comprehensive study of German and American discourses of abortion (Ferree et al. 2002b), Myra Marx Ferree, William A. Gamson, Jürgen Gerhards, and Dieter Rucht examine how the two countries' mediated discourses are linked to their respective dominant democratic theories. In general, German discourses meet the standards of representative liberalism more than American discourses, whereas US discourses come much closer to meeting the criteria set by participatory liberal theory and constructionist theory. German discourses of abortion, with their focus on representation in the state, stress the autonomy of women in public office. In contrast, American discourses clearly lean toward inclusiveness. In terms of empowerment, social movement actors or ordinary nonexperts are more likely to be the speakers in the US discourses; more autonomy and rights language is used. Regarding civility, neither country's discourses are particularly uncivil, probably because the scholars choose mainstream media like *The New York Times* and *Frankfurter Allgemeine Zeitung* (FAZ). The US articles are much more likely to have a dialogic structure – presenting speakers with opposing views and including both core and periphery speakers – than German articles.

In Habermas's ideal civility in the public sphere, emotion has no place. The closest to recognition of emotion in his book is when he discusses "public use of reason" and makes the passing remark that people use not only reason but also contestation ("disdainful disparagement as merely malcontent griping") in mediated discourses (Habermas 1989: 27). After Habermas, the pendulum of modern sociology has swung from a denial of emotion to an upgraded recognition of emotion in various subfields, including cultural sociology (Barbalet 2002).

Cultural sociology has contributed to our understanding of emotion in mediated discourses through some methodological innovations, especially using the massive data available in the media and online discussions. Christopher Bail's study of advocacy organizations' mediated discourses exemplifies this line. In his book *Terrified: How Anti-Muslim Fringe Organizations Became Mainstream* (2015), he found that many once-fringe anti-Muslim organizations dominated media discussions of Islam after 9/11 attacks. Organizations like the Center for Security Policy (CSP) and the Middle East Forum (MEF) beat mainstream organizations like the Council on American Islamic Relations (CAIR), which enjoy more financial resources and larger memberships. The fringe organizations were invited to make comments on Islam and terrorism on the media and summoned as experts to attend congressional hearings even if their academic and professional credentials on the topics were thin and their anti-Islam views extreme.

One might say the rise of anti-Muslim organizations was not surprising because after the 9/11 attacks US society and political arenas generally tended to link the attacks to Islam. Yet this observation is only partially true. While conspiracy theories and ultra-right-wing media spread rumors and hatred toward Muslims, many conservative politicians and public figures, including President George W. Bush, tended to separate Islam from the terrorist attacks. Thus, the rise of anti-Muslim organizations should not be explained by a "resonance" theory, that is, that such organizations resonated with the prevailing political views in the public sphere. Rather, the problem is why such organizations beat more moderate, mainstream, and powerful organizations like CAIR to attract attention and define the public agenda.

One of the explanations Bail offers involves a critical feature of journalism as a profession that tends to report dissenting views, novel messages, and sensational actions. Therefore, journalists were naturally drawn to the anti-Muslim organizations' politically incorrect, rhetorically eccentric, and emotionally melodramatic views about Muslim "complicity" in the terrorist attacks and their tendency to clash with Western civilization. Thus, the "genuinely angry and fearful" anti-Muslim organizations exerted much more media influence than the moderate ones, apparently becoming conservative media outlets' favorites. On a popular Fox News show, MEF leader Daniel Pipes accused Professor Stephen Zunes, the other guest on the show, of blaming the US for the atrocities of September 11. Zunes angrily denied this, and Pipes angrily yelled back. The Fox News host was not an impartial judge of this shouting match: rather, the host thanked Pipes for "doing American parents a favor" by exposing the professor's political bias (Bail 2015: 48). Liberal media outlets, however, reported the conservative media's sensational accusation in critical tones and, in their editorials, even condemned the organizations. Nevertheless, the criticism unintentionally publicized the fringe organizations' message. Negative publicity was also publicity; the fringe organizations won the influence game.

Mainstream Muslim organizations, frustrated and infuriated, first reacted with complex and dispassionate statements to distinguish their reasonable style from the fringe organizations' madness. Later, when such reasonable response was overshadowed, some of the mainstream organizations used equally angry messages to counter the attacks. Others, however, were still concerned with the possible backlash, part of which was that emotional debates would solidify the stereotype of "angry Muslims." Thus, the mainstream organizations either lost ground because they were too restrained or unintentionally helped the anti-Muslim organizations' tactics of escalating the debate and creating a public frenzy. Consequently, the rise of the fringe anti-Muslim organizations has almost undone the efforts of the mainstream organizations and leaders. It has helped create a cultural environment that inspired other eccentric actions, such as the "International Burn a Koran Day," which were picked up by terrorist groups as evidence of Americans' "satanic" nature.

Not all emotions are bad for mediated discourses. In a recent study (Bail et al. 2017), Bail and his associates ask how both reasonable and emotional debates work, in what conditions, and which one works better. The cases are from organizations that advocate for care for autism and human organ donations, two pro-social, less controversial causes. The researchers found that both emotion and reason work, depending on how the conversation style shifts and how the organizations seize the opportunities when the shifts happen. For example, it is a good idea for an advocacy organization to use emotional language to engage in a public debate when the debate has been dispassionate for a long period of time; by the same token, a cool, reasonable voice will stand out when everyone else appears too passionate.

Other scholars also suggest that emotions perform positive functions for mediated discourses, sometimes in counterintuitive ways. In her study of some women-led movements of nineteenth-century America, Eyal Rabinovitch argues that a gendered discourse of affection and compassion enabled women to engage in public activities and have their voices heard in the public sphere (Rabinovitch 2001). In that period, the dominant ideal of "true womanhood" comprised several emotional-virtuous characteristics, such as piety, purity, submissiveness, and domesticity, which contrasted with the features of manhood, such as aggression, self-interest, and so on. More important, these virtues were connected to nationhood in a commonly accepted ideal of "republican motherhood."

Today's readers have good reasons to frown upon these claims, which apparently constituted a gender stereotype. But in that particular context, the stereotype provided women with otherwise unavailable means for direct engagement in the public sphere. For example, on behalf of "virtuous" causes and as "helpless victims" of injustice and men's licentious actions, women disseminated opinions in print and contributed to various moral movements, including the religious revivalism of the Second Great Awakening, the anti-prostitution position of the Moral Reform movement, the abolition movement, married women's property rights, and temperance. The women activists also resorted to emotions rather than reasons, such as continuous public prayer and weeping, to compel men to show contrition.

This historical process, Rabinovitch argues, challenges both Fraser's and Alexander's public sphere theories. Fraser, in her criticism of Habermas, as discussed earlier, emphasizes the inequality and multiplicity of publics instead of a single public sphere but does not see the possibility of marginal groups' use of the existing symbolic structure for expanding their public engagement. Alexander, in Rabinovitch's view, rightly understands this, but he does not pay much attention to the existence of multiple, conflicting codes – for example, the motherhood code is on the emotional and even dependent side of the code, which is "polluted" and thus negative for the culture of democracy. But in the particular historical context, it performed the function of integrating marginal groups. Note that Rabinovitch's argument has inspired later studies of hybrid codes, especially the theory raised by Lo and Fan, but Rabinovitch's interesting point is that hybrid codes exist not only in non-Western societies but also in Western civil societies.

Another way to think about the rational and emotional discourses in the public sphere is that we might be talking about different *publics* instead of a single public sphere. Different publics perform different functions – sociable interactions, information exchange, political discussions, and a mix of all these – and thus form different styles and norms of discourses. Discourses in some publics may be more emotional than others; some types of emotions may be the norm for some publics but not for others. An immediate test of this argument is to visit www.nextdoor.com, a "virtual neighborhood" website, on which neighbors of local communities exchange information and discuss local issues, such as searching for lost pets, recommendations for podiatrists, complaints about stolen Amazon packages, zoning issues in the city, calls for consumption at local restaurants which suffered from the COVID-19 crisis, and so forth. Participants in this online local public consciously shut the door on national political issues. In November 2020, I saw on my Nextdoor neighborhood – a community in Atlanta, Georgia – that someone complained about his less popular presidential campaign signs being stolen. A few others immediately responded: "liberals did it!" But the discussion was quickly hushed by others as inappropriate. This was one of the very few political discussions I saw on my Nextdoor app. Most of the discussions are calm, friendly, and reasonable. Even complaints and expressions of frustration about the local governments are targeted at specific government bureaus and their policies instead of extending to partisan politics.

This calmness, however, did not reflect the political situation at the time. In the presidential election in November 2020 and, later, two Senate runoffs in January 2021, Georgia was in the spotlight: a battleground, slightly Republican-leaning state that turned "blue" (Democratic) in both races. A few months before the election, Ahmaud Arbery, a young Black man in Georgia, was shot to death while jogging by white residents who believed he had stolen things from a local house, which was proven an unfounded accusation. In another case a drunk Black man was shot by two white police officers when he seized the officers' electroshock guns. Protests broke out. Right after the election, upon the request of the defeated Trump campaign, the ballots of the presidential election were audited and recounted. Trump, Republican politicians, and Trump supporters repeatedly claimed that there was "fraudulence" in the election and pressured local election managers to change the election results in their favor. These efforts received surprisingly emotional pushback from the local officials in charge of election management, who were also Republicans but attempted to protect their professional integrity from partisan politics. These intense social, racial, and political tensions were in sharp contrast to the "nextdoor.com harmony."

This colloquial observation corroborates a systematic study by Andrew J. Perrin and Stephen Vaisey. They found similar multiple publics and different styles of discourses in their systematic study of more than 1,000 letters to the editors of the *Greensboro News and Record*, a local newspaper in Greensboro, North Carolina (Perrin and Vaisey 2008). Writers of these letters – ordinary residents of the city – have different audiences and expectations of mediated discourses in their mind and thus consciously adopt different styles. Discussions of local issues are reasoned, conciliatory, while discussions about political issues beyond the local level get more confrontational and emotional. A legitimate explanation is that Americans very much cling to the image of their local communities as "small town" with its corresponding deliberation style, as my previous discussions have shown, and, therefore, talk about local issues with reason and composure. The national mediated discourses were supposed to be more self-interested, inflammatory.

Another important finding in the cultural sociology of civil society is that mediated discourses may take on the features of "drama." "Making a drama" is often seen as manipulative, irrational, and not good for democracy. Nevertheless, cultural sociologists argue that most, if not all, mediated discourses have dramatic features. This certainly does not mean that mediated discourses are little more than charades put on by evil-intentioned corporations and pundits. Rather, it means that mediated discourses attempt to persuade people through arranging and performing the theatrical components we often see in real dramas, such as plays, soap operas, and movies, rather than through Habermas's rational-critical discussions (Goffman 1959: 15; Schechner 2002: 28). What we see in plays is the same cultural logic and structure we use to perceive our social world. In this sense, the dramatic theories are not very far from our everyday notion that "the whole world is a stage."

Using this dramatic perspective, Philip Smith and Nicolas Howe study climate change as a topic in mediated discourses. This scientific topic takes on a certain set of "dramatic" properties once it moves from the realm of science to the public sphere, in narrative genres like reports, debates, documentaries, forums, and so on (Smith and Howe 2015). The underlying cultural logic of the discourses determines which performance will be more successful and effective. For example, the 1997 Kyoto conference on climate did not inspire much public attention to the issue, mostly due to the technical nature of the reports on the conference. Later mediated discourses took on an apocalyptical tone and raised awareness of the issue. A *Time* magazine article aptly links the warning about the dire climate future with biblical fables: "This year the earth spoke, like God warning Noah of the deluge. Its message was loud and clear, and suddenly people began to listen, to ponder what portents the message held" (Smith and Howe 2015: 59). This apocalyptic dramatic narrative was also effectively used in Al Gore's 2006 documentary *An Inconvenient Truth*, which turned an otherwise dull presentation by a dull politician into an intense moral drama. In the documentary, scientific findings were combined with images and narratives about floods, hurricanes, collapsing icebergs, horrific droughts, and so on. This dramatic analysis certainly does not claim that climate change is a hoax; rather, it shows that to effectively engage in mediated discourses, advocacy narratives of an idea must dovetail with the underlying cultural logics of the society.

Similarly, Ronald Jacobs studies how two newspapers in Los Angeles covered the Rodney King beating case by adopting different genres, plots, and characters (Jacobs 1996). In 1991, Rodney King, an African American man, was chased by police officers for dangerously speeding on a highway. After being forced to stop, King was severely beaten by three police officers, and the beating was videotaped by a bystander. After the video was released to local television, public opinion exploded over the police brutality but subsided after the release of the Christopher Commission

Report, which investigated the issue. In 1992, the not-guilty verdict of the four indicted police officers triggered a large-scale protest and riot in LA.

At different stages of this crisis, two LA newspapers, the *Los Angeles Times*, a mainstream newspaper, and the *Los Angeles Sentinel*, an influential newspaper in the local African American community, adopted different theatrical "genres" to depict the complex tensions and conflicts in the event. The *Los Angeles Times* reported the early stage of the crisis using a "romance" genre. The heroes of the romance were Mayor Bradley and the City Council, who publicly called for LAPD (Los Angeles Police Department) Chief Daryl Gates ("antihero") to resign because he refused to hold the officers accountable. The *Los Angeles Sentinel*, in contrast, also used the "romance" genre, but in their stories, the active, unified Black community took the role of heroes who demanded justice from the antiheroes (LAPD). The grand jury investigation, which later led to the indictment of the officers and the eventual "not-guilty" verdicts, was not a major narrative in either newspaper, mostly because it did not fit well into the dominant genres of the papers: no heroes were involved, and the problems were still left unresolved. Eventually, a new hero emerged in a new narrative: the Christopher Commission, an independent commission composed of figures from the local civil society, including lawyers, professors, executives, and former officials. The Commission and its final report were cast in a heroic light, with Gates and LAPD as the antiheroes again. In the *Los Angeles Sentinel*, the "tragedy" genre was also important: the Black community as a whole was depicted as a suffering hero, the victim of insurmountable structural power (in this case, white supremacy and police brutality).

If one could be persuaded relatively easily that advocacy narratives and newspaper reports are performative, many people would be hard-pressed to believe that scientific research papers are as dramatic as literary texts. Joseph Gusfield presents a brilliant, counterintuitive analysis of the performative aspect of the scientific texts widely used in mediated discourses to identify and define social problems (Gusfield 1981). Gusfield's analytical tool is Kenneth Burke's "pentad": *agent* (the actor), *agency* (the tools, objects or "props"), *purpose, scene* (background or setting), and *action* (Burke 1945). These components and their interrelations in a narrative constitute what Burke terms the "grammar of motives" – a pattern of explanations. For example, should a problem be explained by the involved people's characteristics (agent) or the material resources (agency)?

In his subtle and meticulous analysis of scientific papers like "Identification of Problem-Drinking among Drunken Drivers," Gusfield shows that those journal articles cloak their "grammar of motives" in seemingly neutral, scientific analyses. Take the title as an example. It presumes a type of drivers as "drunken drivers" as opposed to "social drinkers" or "responsible drinkers" – attributing the drinking-driving problem to individual drivers' characteristics. Such scientific papers can be – have been – easily used by other mediated discourses to launch a moral crusade on "drunken drivers" with a not-so-subtle allusion to those drivers' ethnic, class, and religious identities. This analysis also has policy implications. For example, if policymakers admit that we cannot realistically prevent all human beings from indulging in alcohol, then the focus should shift from "drunken drivers" (agent) to other components of the drama to minimize the harms of this enjoyable indulgence. If the focus is on "agency," then probably we need better seat belts and other safety equipment in cars. If the focus is on "scene," then probably we should not allow bars opened in big outlets that can be accessed only by highways.

Drawing on a similar dramatic approach, Martin de Santos reveals that statistics, which represent rationality and science, are often used in melodramatic ways in mediated discourses (de Santos 2009). In his study of Argentina's obsession with the obscure "country risk index" (an index that measures risk of investing or lending in a country), he argues that the number becomes a collective representation of multiple meanings, even a "fact-totem." The country risk index is ranked by country and announced on a daily basis, and thus it creates a constantly renewed melodrama of national competition that is used for various rhetorical purposes. One of the dramatic functions is to express the people's disappointment with the government's dismal economic performance. In the public discourses, Argentina's number is often compared to Burundi, Nigeria, or any African country which is ranked as the alleged No. 1 highest-risk country; or, in a cartoon, compared to the USSR. Yes, you read it right, and that's precisely the point: the USSR doesn't exist any more, and Argentina is the worst now. The essence of the fact-totem is twofold: it creates a simplified narrative which reduces everything to numbers, and exactly because of this simplification, the numbers include many symbolic meanings. Readers certainly can relate this case of country risk index to many other statistic dramas, from college ranking via GDP per capita to, most recently, the number of COVID-19 infection cases.

3

Culture in Associational Life

Ordinary men and women, some previously active in politics and others with civic experience under their belts, take voluntary initiatives to make events happen and run meetings. Without pay, they pitch in to do everything from setting up chairs and handing out leaflets, to arranging for speakers, putting out newsletters, and preparing refreshments. At ... meetings, people ask questions and make comments after a speaker has finished his or her presentation. And when groups discuss priorities and decide how to divvy up tasks, quite a few ordinary women and men step up to chair a task force or carry on a key duty. [The] ... meetings have the same "let's pitch in and get it done" air about them as clubs and lodges and church societies throughout America's past as "a nation of joiners."

You wouldn't be surprised if I told you this paragraph – with the name of the association omitted in ellipsis – is from Alexis de Tocqueville's classic *Democracy in America*. It seems to perfectly corroborate Tocqueville's famous description of American associational life: "Americans of all ages, all conditions, and all minds are constantly joining together in groups" (Tocqueville [1840] 2004: 595).

But it is not. It comes from a book by Theda Skocpol and Vanessa Williamson, two contemporary scholars, on the Tea Party movement, a fiscally conservative movement in the United States in recent decades (Skocpol and Williamson 2012: 198). The movement attracted libertarians, social conservatives, and right-wing populists, who were mostly white, married, and older than 45

(2012: 23). Their ideas and ideologies were on the far right of the political spectrum. They made a clear-cut distinction between "hardworking Americans" – mostly themselves – and "freeloaders," whom they implicitly or explicitly equated with Blacks, Latinos, Muslims, and immigrants. Some put a sarcastic bumper sticker on their car: "Keep Working! Millions on Welfare Depend on You!" (Skocpol and Williamson 2012: 67). Thus, they opposed programs that help low-income people or provide subsidies for healthcare. They also openly expressed their distrust in expertise, their idealization of a free market, and their hatred toward the "mainstream media."

Many would hesitate to regard Tea Party associations as part of American civil society. Nevertheless, the Tea Party associations tick all the boxes of a textbook definition of civil association: citizens voluntarily organize themselves into a group to pursue common goals relevant to the improvement of the society according to their view of an ideal society. Many Tea Partiers Skocpol and Williamson met had already developed civic skills in their previous civic engagement, including being "Girl Scout moms," active members of churches, and participants in political campaigns. In terms of gender equality, contrary to the prevalent conception, women played an important role in the Tea Party.

The case of Tea Party associations speaks to the theme of this chapter, the significance of culture for a deeper understanding of associations, a major component of civil society. At the heart of Tea Party associations is a cultural paradox, largely resulting from the discrepancies among several cultural aspects of associational life: culture as formally stated goals an association pursues, culture as a norm of interaction among members of the association, and culture selectively used in their actions. When the Tea Partiers interacted with other members of their associations, they followed the norms of tolerance, solidarity, and equality. They also apparently learned skills to self-govern their activities for a public purpose. They selectively used the culture of democracy but clearly stated that their goal was to pursue and protect "liberty," a word central to their "manifesto" *Give Us Liberty* (by Dick Armey and Matt Kibbe) and various slogans. This upholding of liberty is consistent with the conservative interpretation of Tocqueville that local associations protect liberty from a central-izing state. Nevertheless, the Tea Party associations avoided words like "tolerance." The norm of civility – solidarity, tolerance, and equality – in interactions among themselves was not extended to people outside their groups. Their attitudes toward outsiders were infamously intolerant, even xenophobic and racist. Their explic-itly exclusionary rhetorics and practices are the reason that many exclude them from "civil society."

Nevertheless, the Tea Party associations are hardly an excep-tion. Cultural paradoxes exist in other associations, though in different ways. Associations with explicitly progressive goals may have hierarchical and even authoritarian internal norms. Therefore, including only associations with progressive goals and claims in the concept of "civil society" is too narrow in scope and too normative in approach to effectively present the complexity of real-world civil societies. Cultural sociology treats both progres-sive and conservative associations as part of civil society but does not believe that whether a particular association is or is not part of civil society is a terribly important question. Rather, cultural soci-ology empirically analyzes how associations selectively use, adapt, and challenge the culture of democracy and how different cultural aspects – culture in structure, action, and interaction – constitute paradoxes and contradictions in associational life.

Tocqueville as a Cultural Sociologist

Alexis de Tocqueville can be seen as a pioneer of the cultural sociol-ogy of civil society. Contrary to some contemporary interpretations of his thought, Tocqueville never argues that association member-ship and social ties can automatically convert into a civil society as the social foundation of democracy. Rather, throughout *Democracy in America*, Tocqueville gives primacy to cultural factors, such as feelings, ideas, mentality, attitudes, and so on, and emphasizes their indispensable role in shaping associational life as well as the civic skills and habits that can be nurtured and developed in that life (Schleifer 2012). He defines these cultural factors as *mores*, "the whole moral and intellectual state of a people" (Tocqueville [1840] 2004: 331). The mores include "habits of the heart," which roughly refers to commitment, beliefs, feelings, and other "emotional" components of mores, and "habits of the mind," a less-used phrase, which refers to ideas and opinions. In the current literature, scholars tend to use the "habits of the heart" to refer to both the "heart and mind" in Tocqueville's original theory.

For Tocqueville, democracy is a cultural concept. In most places in his book, Tocqueville uses "democracy" interchangeably with "equality" (Schleifer 2012). Equality is represented in not only wealth, properties, ranks, hereditary privileges, education, and so on, but also in egalitarian attitudes and beliefs that everyone deserves to be treated equally under a political institution. Nevertheless, Tocqueville is a cautious observer rather than an enthusiastic advocate for equality. In an alarming tone which might surprise many modern readers, he states (Tocqueville [1840] 2004: 787): "Equality in fact produces two tendencies: one leads men directly to independence and can drive them all the way to anarchy in an instant, while the other leads by a longer, more hidden, but also more certain path to servitude."

Why does equality lead to "servitude"? First, equality may help a *tyranny of the majority*. If everyone is presumed equal on everything, even intelligence, then, Tocqueville argues, a reasonable deduction is that "there is more enlightenment and wisdom in an assembly of many than in the mind of one, or that the number of legislators matters more than the manner of their selection" (Tocqueville [1840] 2004: 284). The problem is, what if the minority are right? What if the majority decide through an open vote to pass an unjust law to expel some minority groups from the society? Second, ironically, equality may fuel excessive *individualism*. An equal society tends to produce equally weak individuals, who are isolated and apathetic, and thus do not intend to develop common bonds. This leads to the third of Tocqueville's nightmares: the equal, weak, atomistic, mediocre individuals could serve as a social basis for a centralizing state. The individuals are unable to counter the Leviathan they elect through the majority principle.

On this matter, Tocqueville's worry anticipated the theory in the twentieth century that "mass society" with atomistic individuals was a hotbed for totalitarianism (Arendt 1968).

These warnings do not mean Tocqueville longs for the good old days when aristocrats ruled society with their unparallel power, wealth, and culture. A careful reader can certainly sense Tocqueville's ambivalence toward aristocracy. For example, he suggests that aristocratic elements in a society, when concentrated in the legal profession, can prevent the mistakes made by the passion-intoxicated majority. This ambivalence is also evident in some of his statements about equality, like this one: "Equality is *less lofty, perhaps*, but more just, and its justice is the source of its grandeur and beauty" (Tocqueville [1840] 2004: 833 italics added). One might reasonably relate this ambivalence to his background as a descendant of an aristocratic family who suffered much in the French Revolution. His great-grandfather, a reformist thinker who served as Louis XVI's legal counsel when the king was on trial, was executed. And his parents barely escaped death on the scaffold.

Nevertheless, Tocqueville the scholar rather than Tocqueville the aristocrats' descendant makes a calm, visionary argument about equality: no one, no nation, could prevent this trend of equalization, and it's better to work out a smart way to avoid its disastrous outcomes and pursue the better future it might lead to. He argues that it is within our power "to decide whether equality will lead [us] into servitude or liberty, enlightenment or barbarism, prosperity or misery" ([1840] 2004: 834). In sum, Tocqueville's ultimate goal is liberty, not democracy, or at least not democracy as he defines it. Democracy was the leveling trend of modern societies but could bring about perils that endanger liberty. The solution is to strengthen associations as communities, which can promote, as he quotes John Winthrop, "civil and moral liberty that finds its strength in union." "We must defend in all circumstances and if necessary risk our life for" this civil and moral liberty (Tocqueville [1840] 2004: 48).

This civil and moral liberty strengthened in union is at the heart of Tocqueville's civil society theory. It is Tocqueville's *culture of democracy*. Its historical epitome was the self-governing community based on religion, or more precisely, Christianity, fundamental mores for early European immigrants to America. "Liberty looks upon religion as its comrade in battle and victory, as the cradle of its infancy and divine source of its rights. It regards religion as the safeguard of mores, and mores as the guarantee of law and survey for its own duration" ([1840] 2004: 49).

If we do not pay sufficient attention to this cultural aspect, Tocqueville can be easily misread and misunderstood, as he has often been, as a theorist who advocates for the automatic democratic functions of associations. The aforementioned quote – "Americans of all ages, all conditions, and all minds are constantly joining together in groups" (Tocqueville [1840] 2004: 595) – does not reflect Tocqueville's view unless it is combined with another famous sentence of his: "[In associations] feelings and ideas are renewed, the heart expands, and the human spirit develops only through the reciprocal action of human beings on one another" ([1840] 2004: 598). Central to this statement is "feelings and ideas," that is, culture.

Social Capital as a Cultural Concept

"Neo-Tocquevillianism," an umbrella label attached to several loosely connected strands of scholarship, is often depicted as an approach that draws a simplistic formulation from Tocqueville's theory, that is, a direct link between associations and democracy. This is a valid criticism of many studies under this label, but a careful reading of some significant works may suggest that such criticism may not always be fair.

Among the "neo-Tocquevillian" scholars, Robert Putnam, an American political scientist, might be the most famous. He specifies Tocqueville's idea about the benefits of associational life for democracy in a highly operational social scientific concept, *social capital* (Putnam et al. 1993; Putnam 2000). Social capital, Putnam argues, includes "connections among individuals – social networks and the norms of reciprocity and trustworthiness that arise from them" (Putnam 2000: 19). If a community has more local associations, such as PTAs, neighborhood watch groups, and even purely recreational ones like bowling groups, this community has a higher amount of social capital.

Why? Because through frequent associational activities, people know each other well and build trust relationships among themselves. The more actively you as a parent volunteer for sports meets at your children's school, the more likely other parents see you as a trustable person. You often cover other parents' duties at those meets when they have other pressing commitments, and they may do you a favor later when you have to stay home to take care of your sick kids. These mutual helpings and the high level of trust built in the PTAs can be "transferred" to other occasions of associational life. For example, when the township government plans to invite a corporation to open a new grocery store, residents unhappy about the plan quickly organize themselves through their existing networks like PTAs and pick someone they trust to petition the government. The more connected they are through other activities, even if the activities are nonpolitical, the more they trust each other and the more efficiently they participate in public activities. In other words, in Putnam's theory, "social capital" is possessed by the community – not by individuals – and can be "accumulated" in associational activities and "invested" in the collective participation in democratic governance. Therefore, an easy way to identify a healthy democracy is to count the number of associations in a community or a country and ask members if they trust their neighbors or their compatriots in general. The social capital theory specifies some key benefits voluntary associations produce for democracy, such as protecting liberty, nurturing the art of association, and developing the "habits of the heart" (Putnam 2000: 338–41).

It should be emphasized that Putnam's social capital is a *cultural* concept. The core of the concept includes not just the scale or density of networks but also two cultural dimensions: culture as *attitudes* and *values* of the individual members ("mores") and culture as *norms* of interaction such as trust and reciprocity. Both dimensions constitute the "public good" in a group or community. This notion is rooted in the *civic culture* tradition in political studies that emphasizes citizens' attitudes, moral commitments, and trust as the social foundation of a healthy democracy (see chapter 4). In *Making Democracy Work*, Putnam pays tribute to Tocqueville: "Tocqueville highlights the connection between the 'mores' of a society and its political practices. Civil associations, for example, reinforce the 'habits of the heart' that are essential to stable and effective democratic institutions" (Putnam et al. 1993: 11). In *Bowling Alone*, he even explicitly says that social capital is the social scientific analog of "fraternity" – that is, "solidarity," a more gender-neutral term used in this book – one of the key elements in the culture of democracy (Putnam 2000: 351–63; also see Newton 2001). Tolerance, trust, and reciprocity constitute this solidarity, without which a healthy democracy with effective governance is impossible.

Putnam uses this theory to answer empirical questions. The first is: "Why do some democratic governments succeed and others fail?" His site is Italy, where there are significant regional differences in terms of government performance: the regional governments in the north are generally more responsive to the demands of their constituents and more effective in using limited resources to address those demands (Putnam et al. 1993). This variation also exists among the local governments in the same region. Putnam explains this variation in governance by the difference in the strengths of "civic communities," that is, their social capital. In the civic communities with more effective governments, people are more interested in public issues, are more devoted to public causes, tend to form horizontal bonds among citizens rather than the vertical bonds based on authority and dependency, have higher levels of trust, and are more likely to join civil associations that embody those norms and values.

In his later book *Bowling Alone* (Putnam 2000), Putnam returns to the US but paints a bleaker picture of declining social capital since the 1960s. Fewer people voted at the booths. Fewer participated in political campaigns. Memberships of civic organizations, particularly the face-to-face ones, generally plummeted. Fewer parents joined PTAs. There were even fewer bowling groups: people tend to go "bowling alone." Not a nation of joiners any more – rather, what he saw in the late 1990s was a nation of loners. This book joined other books in the "Why-is-American-democracy-in-such-a-mess?" genre and came out at the right time, when Americans were disillusioned with "end-of-history" optimism and worried about the future of American democracy.

Putnam's empirical studies, however, do not fully realize the potential of his cultural concept of social capital. In both books, Putnam does not directly study the cultural aspect of social capital – attitudes and norms that represent solidarity and trust. Instead, he takes for granted that the cultural aspect automatically forms when people are engaged in associational life. Thus, an otherwise reasonable argument that runs from associations to democracy through the mediation of the cultural aspect is reduced to a direct correlation between associations and democracy.

Yet it is exactly this simplified, "minimal-culture" correlation that made Putnam popular, whereas the nuances in the original work are often neglected. As of December 2021, *Bowling Alone* had been cited 75,361 times, and *Making Democracy Work* 53,452, according to Google Scholars; both are among the most cited social science books. The concept of social capital offers academics, policymakers, civil society practitioners, and the public a clear diagnosis and an easy prescription: to revive American democracy, we must enhance social capital by rebuilding civic communities. To do so, "citizens would not need to do anything particularly distasteful in the process, such as becoming involved in politics" (Theiss-Morse and Hibbing 2005: 228). The only thing you need to do is to become a joiner – for example, joining a bowling club.

It is also this simplified argument that provoked controversies. Critics believe Putnam's diagnosis is too linear and his prescription too good to be true. Specifically, critics have pointed out three key limitations (Edwards et al. 2001; Theiss-Morse and Hibbing 2005). First, people are most likely to be "birds of a feather" who join associations with members like themselves, and thus "bonding" ties may not help a generalized trust ("bridging") in civil society. Second, some associations dampen people's enthusiasm for serious political participation. Third, many groups pursue goals that do not necessarily help democracy and are sometimes even antidemocratic (Theiss-Morse and Hibbing 2005). In the next section, I focus on the debate over the third limitation, for it reveals the importance of the goals and meanings of associations.

Goals and Meanings of Associations

Goals and meanings are the missing link in the social capital theory. Some studies generally support the social capital theory but also stress that the goals and meanings that associations pursue will have impacts on their contribution to the community's social capital. For example, in their studies of association and social capital in Norway, Dag Wollebaek and Per Selle confirm the function of voluntary associations in forming social capital. But they also show that leisure-oriented associations do not contribute much to social capital unless their members are also affiliated with semipolitical and political associations (Wollebaek and Selle 2002). In other words, even if you actively participate in a bowling club, you do not contribute much to the social capital of the community unless you and your bowling friends participate in other associations to act on public issues. In this scenario, it is not only the density of networks – the overlapping of different groups – but also the goals of associations that matter, whereas participation in a single group with no explicit goal of contributing to the common good does not make democracy work.

Other studies directly challenge the social capital theory by pointing out the contradiction between culture as a norm of interactions within an association and culture as a goal, value, or meaning that the association pursues. In other words, the solidarity norms developed within associations cannot be extended to social capital in the larger society; rather, they may sustain socially and politically exclusive enclaves. I term this discrepancy the *boundary of solidarity*. The Tea Party associations, which are mentioned at the beginning of this chapter, are examples of such a limited boundary of solidarity. Another example is the American fraternities which mushroomed in the "golden age" of American associations, between the Civil War and World War I.

The fraternal orders, such as the Elks (the Benevolent and Protective Order of Elks), allowed individuals to find their particular, self-segregating social spaces along the lines of race, ethnicity, gender, and class, rather than compelling them to transcend those lines to develop "generalized trust" among different kinds of people (Kaufman 2002). White Americans who believed they were "native" responded by setting up their own fraternities, with members mostly of Protestant origin, such as the Patriotic Order Sons of America. In addition to emotional support and socialization, the fraternal organizations in that period also provided health and life insurance, one of the most enticing benefits for members at a time when public and commercial insurances were scarce. Such exclusivity hid various vices under the surface of solidarity, such as sexism, racial prejudice, interethnic hostility, the dominance of special-interest groups, and so on (Kaufman 2002: 10). Exclusivity instead of inclusivity was the key cultural rule of the fraternities.

Nevertheless, one should not assume that exclusivity only exists in socially enclosed orders like the old fraternities and politically conservative groups like the Tea Party associations. It also, ironically, appears in those associations with more progressive values as their goals, for example the Knights of Labor, an influential workers' organization in the late nineteenth century in the United States (Gerteis 2002). Following the tradition of Republicanism, the Knights of Labor used the rhetoric of "civic virtues" of democratic participation to accommodate Black Americans who were emancipated and actively participated in political activities. But the Knights of Labor barred immigrant workers, especially Chinese workers. Behind this contradiction was the association's cold calculation: Black Americans, who were used by employers as a reserve labor force, could be white workers' allies, whereas new immigrants like the Chinese were already white workers' direct competitors (Gerteis 2002). The complexity in this case shows the need to go beyond simple membership counts and claimed goals to look closely at how associations' actual goals, rhetorics, and meanings are enacted in their actions.

Extreme cases of the boundary of solidarity wrought tragic consequences on millions of people's lives, such as the rise of Nazism in Weimar Germany and fascism in Italy. To explain the rise of the two apparently antidemocratic movements from democracies, Hannah Arendt argues that German society in the Weimar period slid into Nazism because of the rise of a "mass society": a society of people who were indifferent to public affairs, neutral on political issues, and only interested in individuals' success or failure in ruthless competition with others. This mass society emerged from the collapse of major class-based parties and related organizations. The Nazi movement drew supporters from this crowd of alienated individuals who found in Nazism a sense of community and demand of total loyalty to the movement and leaders (Arendt 1968: 305–26).

This well-known view, however, was challenged by many other studies, which show Weimar Germans were not "loners" but "joiners." They were like the Americans Tocqueville described: "whenever three or more Germans gathered, they were likely to draw up by-laws and found an association" (Berman 1997: 407). Max Weber even encouraged his colleagues to study this phenomenon, and the study was to be "starting with the bowling club" – Putnam's favorite emblem of civil society! Numerous local and national associations in Weimar Germany provided citizens, especially the middle class frustrated by the Great Depression, with channels to participate in public life and abandon traditional party politics. The Nazi Party used the dense networks of associations and activists to start a stunningly successful movement, which finally led to the rise of Hitler. The Nazi Party knew associations' effective function of teaching people "arts of association" and consciously used them for training their activists and propagating their ideas (Berman 1997: 420).

Similarly, Dylan Riley found that the rise of Italian fascism was facilitated rather than prevented by strong existing associations. Like their counterparts in the Weimar Republic, the associations helped the movement's recruitment and provided the activists with organizational skills. Riley's study is in stark contrast to Putnam's *Making Democracy Work*. Riley makes the same observations that the regions in the north, such as Lombardy and Emilia-Romagna,

had stronger civil associationism, but this stronger associationism was correlated with more fascist organizations rather than
better democratic governance (Riley 2005). Hyeong-Ki Kwon
confirms this regional correlation in a study of the competition
among socialists and fascists in northern Italian associations
for membership. Fascists finally won the competition because
of their ideological appeal to marginalized groups with various
identities and ideologies, such as unskilled workers, peasants, and
ex-combatants of World War I. Whether associations contribute
to democracy, Kwon observes, depends on how their identities
and interpretative frameworks work in the particular political and
cultural contexts and how the civic solidarity in the association is
used for political purposes (Kwon 2004).

If Nazism and fascism were too extreme cases, then many
other more "normal" associations have the boundary of solidarity problem. Even Putnam himself also admits the importance of
the goals and meanings of associations by mentioning the "unintended vices of social capital." As he analogizes: "The human
capital of biochemists can be used to create lifesaving pharmaceu-
ticals, but also to create biochemical weapons" (Putnam 2002:
9). The more exclusive an association's goal is, the less likely the
association can contribute to generalized trust at the society level,
even if the association has a high level of internal solidarity. You
develop emotional bonds with the members of your fraternities,
through communal living, binge drinking, and hazing as the rites
of passage, but this solidarity justifies and reinforces toxic mas-
culinity, class privileges, and even violence. Your neighborhood
association "means a lot" to you, but this association's goal is to
guard your racially and economically segregated neighborhood
through some questionable practices, such as using guns to fend
off "suspicious outsiders." Even if hate-driven atrocity happens
in the process of armed patrolling and then so-called "citizens'
arrest," some would justify the atrocity by their intention to
"defend the community." Other members will testify that the
person who committed the atrocity is a kind and polite guy, an
active member of the PTA, and a "good citizen"; thus, the violence
"does not reflect his character."

Culture in Associations' Action

The publicly stated goals and meanings constitute part of the association's "cultural repertoire." Like musical repertoire, items in the cultural repertoire are available for the associations to use, but they may choose some instead of others. When they use those chosen items in actions, they also must adapt to the actual situations by changing the meanings and improvising new meanings. This view of "culture in action" emphasizes associations' agency in dealing with the demands and challenges in particular situations.

In her study of American voluntarism and the nation-state, Elisabeth S. Clemens turns this otherwise very "Tocquevillian" case – voluntary associations – against neo-Tocquevillianism by stressing the agency of both the state and civil associations in using items in the cultural repertoire to respond to the changing situations (Clemens 2020). In all historical periods since the United States was founded, voluntary associations have not been independent of the state; rather, the state and associations have been engaged in constant interactions in various ways. At the heart of those complex interactions was a cultural paradox: organized benevolence generated resources and solidarity in support of nation-making and state-building, but such solidarity may create relations of dependence and expectations of gratitude, which may threaten civic equality and the liberty of citizens.

Private charity organizations dealt with this cultural paradox in different ways in different historical periods, responding to the state's various agendas and demands. A pivotal historical moment was Franklin D. Roosevelt's New Deal period, in which civic benevolence was mobilized to support the state's national solidarity in response to the Great Depression. Private charity was clearly not up to the task of relieving a huge population of the unemployed, and thus the relief program was dominated by the federal government. The FDR administration dealt with the cultural paradox between governmental aids and individuals' dignity by redefining the concept of "relief" as a "right" to which a citizen was entitled. Thus, the relief program incarnated reciprocity and was viewed as a "gift" given by other citizens through their taxes. Receiving such a gift did not harm one's dignity because it was not "charity," which implied a condescending giving relationship from winners to losers.

This cultural justification and the state's dominance compelled the private charities to change their strategy and rhetorics. Because the private organizations provided a smaller amount of funds, they tended to emphasize their ability to provide individualized services to those whose needs and situations were not met by the mass distributions of funds. Thus, their self-definition leaned toward being a "helper" who could improve the quality of government programs. In return, the FDR administration welcomed and mobilized private charity, not only using it as an ally in alleviating the crisis but also redefining the charity work in national solidarity terms. Consequently, the state and the private charities converged in their collective response to the economic crisis, not only organizationally but also culturally. They framed donating and volunteering as a moral duty of citizens; receiving relief was not the conduct of a pitiful person reliant on others but an honorable action to practice one's right, and all these were merged in the national solidarity notion which was needed in the time of crisis.

Clemens's important study goes beyond the simplistic causation from generalized trust to democracy consolidation in several ways. First, it points out the intrinsic tensions between different elements of the culture of democracy, especially liberty and solidarity. Second, such tensions may have different features and functions in different historical contexts. Third, good governance may rely on a vibrant civil society, but it takes much work from both the state and civil society to adapt to each other in actions and cultural expressions.

Associations also endeavor to reconcile their own views with the diverse cultures in the civil society they are embedded in. For example, Ruth Braunstein studies how two civic groups, a liberal group "Interfaith" and a Tea Party group the "Patriots," deal with internal and external diversity by using different elements in the culture of democracy (Braunstein 2017). For the

"Patriots," whose members are mainly Tea Partiers, internal diversity is not a major issue, but the key members of the group, who are Christians, still carefully incorporate Christianity into their activities without being religiously stringent in a group in which one-third of the members are not Christians. Their way to achieve this end is to use ideas similar to "civil religion" – a set of political-moral values expressed in the language of Christianity. Like the Tea Partiers described by Skocpol and Williamson, they all emphasize "liberty," especially the liberty notion in the original texts of the American Revolution, such as the Declaration of Independence and the Constitution. They sing "God Bless America," emphasize "one nation under God" in the Pledge of Allegiance and "endowed by their Creator" in the Declaration of Independence – meanwhile criticizing Obama's omission of the phrase when quoting the Declaration. Nevertheless, they do not do collective prayers because they, following the conservative political commentator Glenn Beck, believe prayers are individuals' actions. God is not just the source of virtues but also the source of individuals' rights and liberty.

"Interfaith," in contrast, emphasizes inclusion, another typical element in the culture of democracy, and enacts this inclusion in its practices, such as "bridging cultural practices," which is not intended to produce sameness but to "organize difference," including finding a common position, signaling openness, enacting rituals and symbols known to all members, highlighting their shared characteristics, and celebrating differences. A common bridging cultural practice is "interfaith prayers." A member of the clergy calls for everyone to pray in their own religious traditions: "If you are Jewish, stand for Adonai. If you are Muslim, stand for Allah. If you are Christian like me, stand for Jesus" (quoted in Braunstein 2017: 100). Also, group members are instructed to learn a certain prayer that might be different from their own. Sometimes the prayer removes explicit religious expressions from a specific tradition, or it will incorporate nonreligious texts such as social activism and poetry.

Culture as Norms of Interaction in Tiny Publics

"Culture" in associational life also means the norms, rules, conventions, and customs that sustain the order of face-to-face interactions within and between civil associations (Lichterman 2005). In this sense, culture is what Gary Alan Fine terms *idioculture* or *group culture*, which

> consists of a system of knowledge, beliefs, behaviors, and customs shared by members of an interacting group to which members can refer and that serve as the basis of further interaction. Members recognize that they share experiences, and these experiences can be referred to with the expectation that they will be understood by other members, thus being used to construct a social reality for the participants. (Fine 1987: 125)

Group culture functions for members of a group to maintain the *interaction order* among them – that is, accepting each other's projected self-images and definitions of a situation and keeping their interaction going. Interaction order, thus, is the meso-level solidarity within the group, and group culture defines this solidarity (Fine 2021). Similar concepts from the same interactionist perspective include *group styles* or *speech norms* (Eliasoph and Lichterman 2003; Lichterman and Eliasoph 2014).

When this theoretical perspective is applied to civil society, it revolves around a crucial concept: *tiny public*, that is, a group with "a recognizable interaction order and culture that strives to play a role within a civic structure" (Fine 2021: 14). Internally, a tiny public has the natural tendency to maintain the order within the group; externally, numerous tiny publics constitute the foundation of civil society through their concerted effort as well as conflicts and clashes. In sum, the concept of "tiny public" simultaneously examines culture, interaction, and group in civil society and provides a theoretical tool for civil society at its meso level, that is, groups, associations, and their networks.

From this theoretical perspective, Tocqueville's idea of the "art of association" can be seen as an art of maintaining the interaction order among members of the association in their pursuit of collective goals. This interactionist reinterpretation of Tocqueville can find textual evidence in *Democracy in America*. For example, Tocqueville argues that to participate in associations, especially political associations, one needs to discover

> *how order is maintained* where large numbers of people are involved, and how those large numbers of people can be made to march in step and according to plan toward a common goal. They learn to subject their will to the will of all and to subordinate their individual efforts to the joint venture – all things that are no less necessary to know in civil associations than in political ones. ([1840] 2004: 605–6, italics added)

Tocqueville also asserts that once people develop this art of association in group interactions, they become better citizens, pursue meaningful goals, and build a healthy democracy. In other words, civil associations that pursue the culture of democracy as goals and meanings are also expected to nurture democratic norms of interactions. Two aspects of the culture of democracy – *culture in structure* and *culture in interaction* – should reinforce each other.

Many civil associations' group cultures are in line with their goals. For example, in a study of immigrant rights organizations, Grace Yukich, Brad R. Fulton, and Richard L. Wood show that different group styles of such organizations shape how effectively they keep the immigrants involved in their activities (Yukich et al. 2019). The successful organization in Los Angeles carefully incorporates diverse religious traditions, accommodates the decision-making mode and speech norms that are comfortable for immigrants with lower socioeconomic statuses, and conducts their activities in multiple languages. The unsuccessful one in New York mostly relies on Christian practices without serious consideration of other religions, emphasizes a middle-class, US-based speech norm (such as personal introduction and public speaking), and writes its materials and conducts its activities mostly in English. Thus, the styles and norms of interactions in the New York organization do not constitute a conducive culture for immigrants to be involved. Similarly, in his study of civic groups and democratization in Nigeria, Darren Kew shows that those groups with highly democratic norms of interaction – practicing equality in negotiation, respecting the right of participants to discuss issues, tolerating opposing views, resorting to nonviolent resolution, and so on – tend to actively engage in promoting democracy in the national political system (Kew 2016: 271).

Nevertheless, group cultures are not always in line with the goals and effectiveness of their activities. Dynamics and processes of interactions sometimes shape people's definitions of situations and lead to norms of interactions different from the values they pursue. For example, Nina Eliasoph's study of grassroots civic groups shows that the volunteers in the groups she observed tried very hard to "hide" the public spirit – emphasizing their participation without talking about the issues publicly (Eliasoph 1998). This was particularly true when volunteers were confronted with issues that cannot be changed easily. For example, if a major air polluter in the town caused many schoolchildren's respiratory problems, what many volunteers chose to do was to take care of the children rather than to discuss the pollution issue, let alone take action on it. This led to a shrinking circle of concern but a heightened "can-do" spirit.

In general, civic groups tend to work on easy-fix issues through "plug-in volunteering" – work which focuses on specific tasks, such as helping with children's homework, and requires short-term, sporadic commitment, such as one hour every week. Or, as Eliasoph shows in a later study, groups gradually converge on some "no-brainer" activities, such as picking up litter, gathering food for the hungry, and so on. "No-brainer" projects do not involve discussions of the roots of the problems. But because of their limited but concrete goals, participants' enthusiasm and sense of self-efficacy are nearly guaranteed: "We accomplish a lot!" (Eliasoph 2011: 87–114).

This norm of interaction ("avoiding talking about politics") is rooted in a belief that talking about politics would lead to controversy, which in turn could threaten the group's solidarity and the volunteers' sense of accomplishment. In everyday life, avoiding talking about politics may help smoothen otherwise complicated relations, especially on social occasions, for example, refraining from talking politics at a family reunion dinner, if your opinion-ated uncle recently voted for a different presidential candidate. But in civic engagement, such a tendency to maintain group solidarity sometimes fails to transcend the group boundary to tackle bigger issues. It serves as a wrong solution to the problems which should be solved through changing institutions and politics. For example, volunteers are needed to supervise the playground in the morning before school starts because "parents have to leave for work at 6 or 6:30a.m., and there are no before-school programs even in the elementary schools, so the parents have no choice but to just dump their kids – first graders, second graders, even – on the playground, sometimes before it's even light out, and just hope for the best" (Eliasoph 1998: 47). The parents' volunteering certainly helps those in need, but the mutual help does not solve the long-term problem if no one is asking why the school has no before-school programs and why companies cannot accommodate working parents' schedules. As a result, as Eliasoph argues, serious discus-sions about public issues evaporate from civic engagement.

On some occasions, talking does not evaporate, but the norms of talking in civic groups "filter" the macro-level cultures of democracy. For example, some groups may use expressive indi-vidualism to talk about public-spirited activities ("I do this for my family"); or another group might use sexist, racist language and inappropriate jokes to show their authenticity ("This is who we really are"). Both speech norms are individualistic rather than communal, exclusionary rather than inclusive, uncivil instead of civil. But their purposes are to maintain the interaction order within the group: individualism is encouraged because the group values speeches and voices from various people, and the uncivil language deliberately shows their distance from institutions, companies, and conventions of politics in general (Eliasoph and Lichterman 2003).

The speech norms in associations may also have unintended exclusionary effects along the lines of class, gender, and race. As a group of researchers led by Baiocchi observe (Baiocchi 2013), civic group members often talk "around" issues of inequality, using phrases, stereotypes, euphemisms, and indirect references:

for example, replacing "the working poor" with "really salt of the earth kind of people." A speaker at a group meeting referred to a racially diverse, low-income neighborhood, which happened to be located in a downhill place, as "people down there," and the other members jokingly repeated with a slow pace and low-pitched voice "dowwwwwn therrrre" with laughter to show a tacit understanding of this reference. This exchange relieved the tension due to class disparity and racial differences by not mentioning them (2013: 103). Unsurprisingly, the group's leadership and membership were populated by affluent homeowners. In contrast, groups with social justice as a goal often directly talk about race, gender, and class: for example, in a group meeting, a member demanded that people better see her as a Black woman (2013: 103). Nevertheless, even when these justice-oriented groups use expressions like "working poor" and emphasize their identity as being underprivileged and oppressed, they tend to obscure the differing levels of underprivilege. For example, when an activist claims that "we're all working poor," no one objects, even if the members include Ivy League professors and other professionals (2013: 107).

Some studies offer a more optimistic image. When a civic group expands its scope, identifying as part of a bigger social movement, there might be a turning point in the group culture. For example, Kathleen Blee's study of a group called ALL (Animal Liberation League) shows that such a turning point occurred when the group decided to follow the national movement and campaign against foie gras instead of just meeting and talking about animal rights (Blee 2012). This idea of putting ALL in a larger movement sparked immediate interest, and members no longer viewed their engagement as local or trivial. Rather, they became fluid and expansive, tied to a higher goal and a broader community (2012: 43). The pace of the activities speeded up, as the group wrote letters to restaurants to demand they remove foie gras from their menus. The standards were also changing to be measured against a major movement. When restaurants did not respond to their letters, the group decided to protest in front of the restaurants. The protests led to internal debates and conflicts over issues like the lack of resources, timing, and frequency of the protests. In the confrontations with restaurants, the owners' rude reactions and the patrons' indifference led to the group members' heightened level of emotional confrontation. In this dynamic process, the civic group's understanding and definition of the issues and their tactics evolved as the interactions with the restaurants and among themselves evolved.

Generally along this line of culture as interaction norm, Andrew Perrin offers another theoretical concept to understand the culture of democracy: "democratic imagination," people's imagining about what a citizen can do, including "what is possible, important, right, and feasible" in civic life (Perrin 2006: 2). The democratic imagination, however, is not an individual-level cultural concept. Rather, it is born in conversations with others, mostly in group settings. To illustrate this idea, Perrin uses the focus group method and recruits four groups of civic organizations in each of five different types: Protestant church, Catholic church, labor union, business organization, and sports group. Each of the twenty groups has 4–13 members. Perrin then presents four scenarios to the recruited groups: alleged racial profiling by local police, a politician's malpractice, a local chemical company's violation of environmental regulations, and excessive noise from a recent airport expansion. The group members then discuss together, with the researcher as moderator, whether they want to get involved in the issue and what they would do about it.

The study shows that the type of group influences their democratic imagination, including what logic their argument is based on, what methods of solving the problem they propose, and what resources they use to bolster their arguments. For example, church groups tend to interpret the issues in moral ways, whereas union groups pragmatically highlight their capacity to make a difference. As for methods to solve problems, union groups prefer private methods, such as staying away from problematic situations, whereas business groups favor governmental solutions, such as a representative committee.

"Uncivil Society"?

What worries civil society advocates most in the past few decades is various types of associations under the ill-defined umbrella label *"uncivil society,"* including those associations with values and practices that are believed to deviate from the progressive version of the culture of democracy (Roggeband and Glasius 2020). They are more or less openly illiberal, right-wing populist, anti-immigration, anti-Muslim, and so on. Some theorists believe that "uncivil society" is an unfortunate, unintended consequence of civil society. For example, Andrew Arato and Jean L. Cohen, two renowned theorists of civil society, believe that right-wing populism, a typical idea and practice of "uncivil society," is *in* but not *of* civil society (Arato and Cohen 2017). Right-wing populism is *in* civil society because the openness and equality of civil society facilitate populism by allowing its associational life and open expressions of ideas. It is not *of* civil society because its exclusionary, unequal values contradict what Arato and Cohen believe is the essence of the culture of democracy of civil society, particularly equality and inclusiveness. It is in the latter sense – not *of* civil society – that right-wing populism is regarded as "uncivil."

This label of "uncivil society," however, diverts our attention away from more significant issues. It adopts a narrow notion of "civil society," which is much in line with the progressive version of the culture of democracy. But it fails to see that the culture of democracy is a multivocal, multilayered amalgam of various ideas, values, and norms. Both progressive associations and alleged "uncivil society" associations selectively use and interpret some items in the culture of democracy, such as liberty and equality, to justify their claims. Both share the same cultural paradox in the discrepancy between the values they pursue and the norms of their interactions. Therefore, both should count as part of civil society in its empirical sense.

Nevertheless, the crucial problem is not to argue over who should count as in or out but how to grasp the complexities and paradoxes that are often belied by the simplistic label "uncivil society." Take populism for example. Various populisms, on the left and on the right, are intended to promote equality, inclusion, voice, social justice, and democracy according to their imagining of these values. They emphasize that the members of populist movements are ordinary people who are fed up with the "deep state" or "elites" or "big capitalists." The problem with populism, however, mostly occurs when it exaggerates and reifies this "elite-versus-people" distinction. It defines "the people" as pure and good but elite as corrupt and bad. Moreover, their definition of "the people" is much narrower than normal; they usually claim that "they and they alone represent the people" (Müller 2016: 101). "Outsiders" in any of the populist categorization systems (ethnicity, nationality, citizenship, skin color, and so on) are linked to negative attributes, such as being lazy, greedy, law-violating, uncivilized, rude, and so on (Brubaker 2017). Within the populist associations, nonetheless, the internal norms of interactions might be consistent with the culture of democracy – equality, solidarity, and tolerance, which, however, are not extended to the larger society.

The civil sphere theory (CST) provides a better understanding of the complexity of populism. Alexander argues that populism is triggered by the contrast between the promised values in the mainstream culture of democracy, such as equality, and the unsatisfactory reality, in which social inequality prevails and exclusionary practices are ubiquitous (Alexander 2021). This explanation is compatible with the "cultural backlash" theory (Norris and Inglehart 2019). Where the developed democracies have provided incredible economic security after World War II, the younger generations, especially those who are economically and socially more secure, tend to be more "post-materialist": less concerned with survival, less conformist, more open to new ideas, and more tolerant of outside groups. But this post-materialism triggered a cultural backlash from the older generations who are less economically secure, suffer from global inequality, and feel disoriented by the erosion of traditional values and lifestyles. This cultural backlash was exacerbated by various social, economic factors: outsourcing work from high-income countries to middle-to-low-income countries, the resulting unemployment in the high-income countries, the reverse immigration flow, widespread use of automation and the resulting concentration of wealth in the hands of fewer elites, and so on. As a result, the working class, whites, and men who are left behind by the changes lean toward the right. A prevalent feeling among those people, as Arlie Hochschild aptly describes, is that they feel like "strangers in their own land": they work hard to get into a long line to achieve their dreams but, as they imagine, others – immigrants or minorities or elites – cut into the line and ruin their dreams (Hochschild 2018). Both left and right populisms demand closing the gap between the ideal and the reality, but both are frustrated that the means to achieve this end are controlled by those they perceive as elites.

In short, populism is a misoriented attempt at *civil repair*. In this sense, so-called "uncivil society" is part of civil society in its empirical sense. Thus, within the identity boundaries, members of "uncivil society" learn the "art of association" and develop their "habits of the heart" to make a difference in politics. Their tolerance and equality are interaction norms within "us" instead of "them." The "uncivil" associations also work the binary codes (pure versus polluted; equal versus unequal; fair versus unfair) but set themselves on the positive side and their opponents on the negative side (Alexander 2021). The problem is that this use of the culture of democracy goes too far and, to the extent that it uses exclusionary definitions, creates its own backlash and defeats its own purposes. From the CST perspective, populism, especially right-wing populism, fails to elevate its particularistic goals to universalistic claims. Thus, CST provides an empirically grounded analysis of populism and avoids falling into the usual pitfall of moralist accusations.

4

Culture in Civic Engagement

Neither associations nor the public sphere can exist without citizens' engagement. Yet, for ordinary citizens, to engage in associational life and public sphere discourses is to add another demanding item to their long to-do lists. After working for a whole day, fighting traffic, picking up kids from school, cooking dinner, and washing dishes, one has many legitimate reasons to shun a civic group meeting at 7pm. Participating in serious discourses is also time-consuming and, perhaps more importantly, distressing. Even when digital devices now enable us to log on to Twitter to participate in public discourses at any time or place, debates over controversial public issues can still bring about headache and anger rather than fulfillment.

Nevertheless, numerous people still do volunteering, attend regular group meetings outside their work, engage in serious discussions about their communities and countries, and even travel to other countries to offer help. Those active citizens make civil societies possible. Why do they engage? What motivates them? How do they understand and talk about the meanings of their engagement? What are the effects of their engagement on their views of politics and society, attitudes toward others with different opinions, and skills of self-governing?

All these questions focus on the cultural aspect of *civic engagement*, which can be defined as individuals' involvement in associations or the public sphere to improve their societies according to their notion of a good society. The key to civic engagement is individuals' notion of a good society and their corresponding understanding of the meanings of their actions. One might object that people engage in public activities for various self-interested reasons: getting volunteering hours for college application, hanging out with neighbors, enjoying local fame and stardom, building networks for business purposes, and so on. This is a legitimate objection. But compared to other actions, civic engagement is farther from the cultural expectation based on self-interest. It demands individuals come up with more cultural meanings to explain and justify their actions. "Why are you doing *this*?", a question often posed to civically engaged citizens, in fact, means "Why are you doing *this* if *this* does not bring you tangible benefits and if *this* probably does not lead to any significant outcomes?"

Therefore, individuals often draw on different elements in the prevailing cultural structure about "good society" and "good citizen" to make sense of and justify their engagement. They also develop various ways to deal with the issues that emerge during their engagement process, such as how to address the root causes of some social problems and how to talk to those with completely different political views. Their engagement has varying effects on their views, attitudes, skills, and dispositions. This chapter presents how cultural sociology examines the topics about the cultural aspect of civic engagement.

Civic Culture

The classical notion of civic engagement asserts that democracy needs citizens with civic virtues. In their highly influential study, Gabriel A. Almond and Sidney Verba articulate this notion in their concept *civic culture*, "a pluralistic culture based on communication and persuasion, a culture of consensus and diversity, a culture that permitted change but moderated it" (Almond and Verba 1963: 8). This definition is a typical concept of *culture in structure* because it focuses on the values and patterns defined in a democratic system. Yet Almond and Verba's empirical research examines individual attitudes and opinions. There is no contradiction, however. The essence of "civic culture" is that a political system is "internalized in the cognitions, feelings, and evaluations of its population" (Almond and Verba 1963: 14).

This idea of mutual reinforcement of polity and individuals prevailed in other studies in the 1950s and 1960s: for example, Harold Lasswell's list of democratic personality traits, such as an "open ego," a capacity to share values, trust and confidence, tolerance of multiple values, and so forth (Lasswell 1951: 495). Nevertheless, underneath the surface of its largely confirmatory message about Western democracy, the civic culture concept expressed a prevalent worry about the stability of democracy, the lack of sensible explanations of the atrocities in the two world wars, shock about the rise of fascism and Nazism within democracies, and anxieties about Communism. For this reason, one could regard Theodor W. Adorno et al's *The Authoritarian Personality* (1950) as the "evil twin" of the "civic culture" study.

Almond and Verba placed their hope in what they called "participatory explosion" in democratic countries and the widespread belief that ordinary people could and should become active participants in the political systems. What became empirically important, nevertheless, was whether citizens under democracies could meet the expectations of the ideal civil culture. To explore this question, Almond and Verba conducted a survey with a stratified, multistage probability sample of 5,000 people from five democratic nations: the United States, Great Britain, Germany, Italy, and Mexico.

Their findings showed a significant gap between the ideal and the actual civic cultures in even the most established and stable democratic nations. Some citizens actively participated in public affairs, but many others preferred to take a passive role in politics. Even those active ones held attitudes along the lines of what Almond and Verba termed "parochial" political cultures: they cared less about the political system, the possible change, its impacts, and their own role in politics than about what benefits the political system would bring to them. Thus, in major democracies, such as the US and UK, respondents showed social distrust, isolation, apathy, and disbelief in their competence to change the political systems. Almond and Verba, however, still asserted that one should not worry too much about the discrepancies between the ideal and the reality. "The civic culture, which sometimes contains apparently contradictory political attitudes, seems to be particularly appropriate for democratic political systems, for they, too, are mixtures of contradictions" (1963: 476).

About thirty years later, one of the authors of *Civic Culture*, Sidney Verba, worked with his colleagues to conduct another study of civic culture in the United States, which was reported in *Voice and Equality: Civic Voluntarism in American Politics* (Verba et al. 1995). *Voice and Equality* shares with *Civic Culture* the same goal of explaining citizens' motivations and capacity to participate in civic engagement. It even shares the same overall optimism: for example, the authors find "a great deal of voluntary participation . . . aimed at the common good. Voluntary activity in America is – more often than popular descriptions or social theory might lead us to believe – about civic matters" (Verba et al. 1995: 26–7).

But *Voice and Equality* differs from *Civic Culture* in its focus on inequality among citizens. Whose voices get heard? What social and material conditions shape citizens' motives and capacity for participation? Verba et al. argue that the primary answer to both questions is resources. Underprivileged groups' low interest in politics and lack of a sense of efficacy often result from their lack of resources rather than unwillingness. One may be interested in politics. But if this person is doing three jobs to make ends meet, then he or she has no time for political activities that do not bring food to the table. The more resources (time, money, social connections, and so on) one has, the more likely one will be able to participate in political and civic actions. The more participation one has, the more likely one has better knowledge about politics, develops more interest, holds a stronger belief in his or her influence, and feels an affinity with some political party. If political participation is the way for ordinary citizens to have their voices heard, then their voices should be clear enough to convey effective messages and loud enough to have influence. "Clear enough" needs citizens' knowledge, and "loud enough" needs money, networks, and time.

If you do not have the resources that allow you to speak well, your voice will be neither clear nor loud.

Cultural Repertoires and Individual Interpretations

Both *Civic Culture* and *Voice and Equality* adopt a concept of *culture in structure*, the ideals in the political system, which can be internalized by individuals in their political socialization process. The discrepancies between the ideal and real civic cultures thus can be explained by incomplete political socialization or lack of resources. A solution to the problem, therefore, is to mobilize possible resources to "educate" citizens or let citizens educate themselves through civic engagement.

Cultural sociologists raise serious doubts about this notion of internalized values and the corresponding "over-socialized" individuals. Cultural sociology since the 1970s has emphasized individuals' agency and eschewed the image of culturally "duped" individuals. This new cultural sociology paradigm asserts that the cultural structure of every society always supplies multiple items instead of just one. These multiple items constitute individuals' *cultural repertoires* – as mentioned earlier, like musical repertoires – for individuals to draw from to understand and talk about their actions (Swidler 1986; Wuthnow 1987; Swidler 2001). Another analogy is a *cultural toolkit* from which an individual can choose appropriate and convenient tools for the specific project (Swidler 1986). Moreover, multiple items in a repertoire may be in conflict with each other, and individuals may struggle to balance their choices when talking about why they are doing certain things. Such struggles are particularly difficult when individuals talk about actions like volunteering that do not generate material returns for them.

In the field of civil society, a pioneering study using this conception of culture is *Habits of the Heart* by Robert N. Bellah and his associates – Richard Madsen, William Sullivan, Ann Swidler, and Steven Tipton, then Bellah's students and later prominent scholars in their respective fields (Bellah et al. 2008 [1985]). Bellah et al. interviewed ordinary Americans in several different locations to know how they think about their lives in relation to others in the society, a classic sociological question. Their findings are multifaceted and cover different topics. What is relevant here is how Americans think about fulfilling their responsibilities as good citizens and what their thoughts tell us about the cultural foundation of American civil society. More specifically, Bellah et al. show two countervailing forces in American "mores" or "habits of the heart": Americans' entrenched individualism and their longing for communal life.

These two forces were discussed in Tocqueville's *Democracy in America*. Tocqueville warned about the threat of individualism to democracy (Tocqueville [1840] 2004: 585):

> Individualism is a reflective and tranquil sentiment that disposes each citizen to cut himself off from the mass of his fellow men and withdraw into the circle of family and friends, so that, having created a little society for his own use, he gladly leaves the larger society to take care of itself.

Tocqueville said that democracy based on such individualism "leads him [an individual] back to himself and threatens ultimately to imprison him altogether in the loneliness of his own heart" ([1840] 2004: 587). Such a state of atomistic individuals becomes fertile soil for tyranny, the opposite of democracy. Fortunately, Tocqueville observed, Americans were also a nation of joiners. Their associations defended liberty at the grassroots level.

Bellah clearly shared with Tocqueville the same worry about individualism but was less optimistic about the self-correcting function of associations. *Habits of the Heart* was written in the 1980s as a response to an upsurge of conservativism, which preached the automatic miracle of an unregulated market and attempted to dismantle state apparatuses to pave the way for corporations and individual consumers. Bellah examined individualism in people's mores and explored the social forces that can offset its destructive consequences.

Bellah and his associates found a paradox: the two fundamental aspects of American political culture – citizens as individuals and as joiners – connect in Americans' use of individualism to understand good society and good citizens. Such individualism has two types: *utilitarian individualism*, which maximizes individuals' self-interests, including psychological interests, and regards getting involved in public affairs as a way to gain returns for themselves; and *expressive individualism*, which views involvement in public affairs as a way to express individuals' ideas, preferences, and feelings.

For example, Howard Newton, a car dealer, one of their interviewees, is a case of how utilitarian individualists understand their contributions to their communities. A typical "town father" in Suffolk, Massachusetts, Howard truly believed in individuals' independence and regarded his community service as driven by his self-interest. He was proud of his "personal way" of running his business, meaning knowing and treating his customers as members of the local community, instead of "just buyers," which he believed was how bigger dealers thought about their customers. This personal approach carried over into his involvement in community service. He saw no conflict between his self-interest and the public good: contributing to the community brought him individual gratification; the prosperity of his business depended on the prosperity of his community. This was a classic model of "enlightened self-interest" (Bellah et al. 2008 [1985]: 174):

> In the vocabulary of the town father, the public good is thus defined in terms of the long-range ability of individuals each to get what they have paid for, no more and no less. One's contribution to the community – in time and taxes – is not thought of as a duty but as a voluntary investment.

So far so good. Except the town was no longer the homogeneous, well-integrated town in Howard's imagination and in the myth of American democracy. By the time of the interview, town residents were increasingly diverse. People like Howard gradually but clearly realized that their life and job were inevitably embroiled in the nexus of national and even international changes outside the town. Howard's job, as a car dealer, made him know this. In the 1980s, the American automobile industry was seriously challenged by Japanese automakers. Howard made speeches in the local Rotary Club to advocate for a government loan for Chrysler, the brand he dealt. He justified his advocacy by an argument that individuals, particularly "lazy workers," and associations like unions, rather than the corporation, were responsible for the decline of American automakers. Therefore, a loan to Chrysler or other forms of bailout would prevent "hardworking people" like him from losing jobs and businesses, which, according to his calculation, would cost the government and the society much more money than the loan.

How did Americans living in metropolises view their civic engagement? The image Bellah provided was more complicated than that of small towns. Metropolitan Americans lived among strangers instead of people they knew. Thus, they tended to find people with similar preferences and formed many lifestyle enclaves. Individuals' voluntary choice and preference – the essence of expressive individualism – were at the heart of such a worldview, even when they pursued goals with the public good, from charities in clubs for the wealthy to activism organized by "concerned citizens." They saw their civic engagement as motivated by community concern, but their "community" consisted of self-interested individuals.

Other scholars continue to explore this paradox of individualism and civic engagement but present a more positive image: individualism and commitments to the community are not mutually exclusive; rather, individualism may provide a cultural language for individuals to construct accounts of their engagement in their communities (Wuthnow 1991; Lichterman 1996). Such accounts are certainly not easy. On the one hand, you want to appear "pure" – in other words, the last thing you should say about your volunteering is that you volunteer because you want to use it to develop business networks. On the other hand, if you appear too pure or too "angelic," then you sound phony. Entirely altruistic accounts of motives are abnormal in an individualistic society and would not pass cynical scrutiny.

In a systematic study of American volunteers, Robert Wuthnow found that most Americans he interviewed were struggling to find the balance between their altruistic actions and individualistic language (Wuthnow 1991). A particularly interesting interviewee was John Casey, who regularly volunteered as a member of the rescue squad in a local fire station. Casey contributed a significant number of hours to various forms of volunteering, from teaching workshops to saving people's lives through emergency rescue. He embodied a typical rugged individualism. "I'm the kind of person who likes to be relatively independent of other people," he says. Such a macho individualism could find its origin in the American cultural repertoire, such as the "Lone Ranger" myth, a masked ranger who wandered around and worked alone – except for a Native American sidekick – to kill "bad guys" and maintain the safety of the communities he passed. Every rescue mission was an "ego trip" for Casey: "Going to a fire is an adrenaline rush. It's exciting. Putting on your mask and running into a burning building is a raw, stupendous thrill!" (Wuthnow 1991: 24). Thus, volunteering gave him tremendous personal gratification and an opportunity for therapy to cure his "savior complex."

"I help people so that I myself am emotionally satisfied." This type of individualistic account is logically sound and culturally comprehensible. But what was absent in Casey's account was compassion for others; it was all about himself. This did not mean he was not a compassionate person. Nor did it mean he did a few hundred volunteering rescue missions in a year only to satisfy his ego or cure his savior complex. Rather, this meant that he had difficulty finding the right *language* except individualism to talk about his unusually active engagement. Moreover, when volunteering work was not an adrenaline rush but boring and menial, he continued to do it anyway but failed to come up with a meaningful narrative about his motive. This is the limitation of the individualist account.

Despite all these struggles to reconcile individualism and altruism, volunteering still represents a key component in every cultural framework: hope. Such hope is not superficial; rather, it is a deep-rooted cultural symbol of a wish to make society a better place, a key idea of civil society. Wuthnow says (1991: 233–4):

Volunteer work will save us because it implies hope. It gives us a sense of efficacy, of being able to make a difference. It inspires confidence in the human condition, in the goodness of those who are truly needy and deserve our help. . . . This, as I say, is a hope that lies in the realm of symbolism and myth.

Cultural frameworks in other countries also supply individuals with multiple items in their repertoires to understand and talk about their civic engagement, although individualism may not be as dominant as in the US context and the official ideology of the states may be more influential. For example, in contemporary China, there are at least four influential cultures about civic engagement. The deep-rooted Chinese traditional culture, especially the folk values influenced by Confucianism, highlights one's moral responsibility for family and community. The socialist value system, which has been fading after the Mao era but remains the official political culture, emphasizes one's moral and political obligation to obey the rules set by the state. The new individualism, which is prevalent among the younger generations, encourages individuals to express their own ideas and pursue personal success. Chinese nationalism, which has been heavily used by the post-Mao state to justify its sovereignty, also remains influential among ordinary Chinese who take pride in national identity and are sensitive to outside criticisms.

Chinese citizens mobilize various items in their cultural repertoires to understand, interpret, and discuss their civic engagement. In my study of the volunteers who participated in the rescue and relief effort after the 2008 Sichuan earthquake (Xu 2017), I show a wide range of items the volunteers used to understand their actions. The items included the Buddhist notion of "compassion," national pride and solidarity in front of a catastrophe, and, like the American volunteers, individualism. A typical way of using individualism to talk about their volunteering was: "I volunteered because it made me feel good and satisfied." Take Xiaoli as an example: a young businessman who had just started his own company before the earthquake spent almost all his savings – about 140,000 *yuan* ($20,000) – to purchase relief supplies and donated them to the people affected. He described their financial situation this way: "If [before the earthquake] we still had two bricks, then the bricks were gone, and we had only cinders." But Xiaoli did not regret this; rather, he used a utilitarian language of success to talk about his decision (Xu 2017: 72):

> How many people would use money to do this kind of thing? Also, how many people can use this little money to do such a big thing? Yes, I spent around a hundred thousand yuan, but I collected relief materials worth more than three hundred thousand. From an economic perspective, I made a fortune! Although the materials didn't end up in my hands, it was more than a hundred percent profit! I believe any businessman who can make that kind of profit would be considered successful.

In contrast, the official ideology about volunteering – based on the "spirit of Lei Feng," a model soldier in the 1960s who represented official altruism as well as loyalty to the Party-state – has rendered little meaning for ordinary Chinese citizens. Among my volunteers to Sichuan, very few used the official language. Even those volunteers who were mobilized by state organizations distanced themselves from the official language by emphasizing their spontaneity.

This finding corroborates Anthony Spires's research on volunteering in normal, nonemergency settings. Spires's study shows that ordinary Chinese volunteers often criticize state-organized volunteering activities as "boring," "just a show," "too formalistic," and sometimes too utilitarian instead of being meaningful and emotional (Spires 2018). For example, young students were mobilized by the government to be audiences of sports events that were under-attended. What they did was basically sit together in an area so that the photographer could take a picture to show good attendance even if other areas were nearly empty. Students were organized to visit a nursing home, but only to deliver their gifts to the elderly without having conversations with them, and, probably more important, to take pictures for PR purposes. Therefore, many volunteers felt not only bored but also disillusioned with the government, the school, and even some of their fellow volunteers, who were opportunistic about volunteering – for example, interested in getting recognition and appointing themselves to positions in their volunteer groups to advance their career.

Nevertheless, when the volunteers distance themselves from the official ideology and the prevalent utilitarianism, they find limited options of proper cultural interpretations of their actions. Consequently, they tend to use ambiguous words like "heart" or "faith" without specifying what the words mean. For example, Rundong Ning and David A. Palmer's study of "sacrificial volunteers," who quit their jobs to volunteer teaching at a small school for migrant workers in Beijing, reveals the dilemmas volunteers have when they participate in this "high-cost engagement" (Ning and Palmer 2020). When asked "Why are you doing this kind of thing?" – meaning making bold, if not impulsive, decisions to disrupt their careers – their common answer is a vague statement: "I just follow my heart" (2020: 403): "as long as there is something called faith in your heart, there is a force that guides you to goodness, and you will be willing to go along the direction your heart tells you." But very few volunteers could specify and articulate what the faith in their hearts was. This, as Ning and Palmer argue, demonstrates the absence of an adequate moral language in the cultural framework, leading to volunteers' difficulty in selecting the right cultural items in the framework to talk about their altruistic actions.

This lack of language was even more evident in the fact that many of the sacrificial volunteers do not answer or reflect on the question "why." Here's a Chinese volunteer's expression of frustration and avoidance (Ning and Palmer 2020: 395):

> When I volunteer, I don't feel like talking about my situation with others. I feel that I'm kind of separated from the outside world. I don't know how to tell them about myself. I don't want to hear things like "You're so brave!" or "How can you just do this – what about your future?" I've been thinking about this question and haven't yet found an answer. If others ask me, I get upset. It seems like I'm trying to avoid talking about my volunteering.

Explaining Civic Engagement

Why do some people participate in civic engagement while others do not? Sociologists have identified many factors to explain one's likelihood of engaging and volunteering, including demographics like age and gender, socioeconomic factors like incomes, and social networks (Wilson 2000). Some cultural factors are highlighted in this line of research, albeit sometimes under the label of "psychological factors" (Barrett and Pachi 2019). For example, scholars have identified a key predictor of civic engagement, *political efficacy*, meaning individuals' belief in the possibility that they themselves, organizations, and states can have an impact on politics and meet citizens' demands. There are three different types of efficacy:

> Internal political efficacy is the belief that one understands political issues and is able to participate effectively in political situations; external political efficacy is the belief that politicians and political institutions are responsive to citizens' demands; while collective political efficacy is the belief that a collective group to which one belongs is able to have an effect on political situations. (Barrett and Pachi 2019: 29)

All of these are positively correlated with individuals' civic engagement. The more you believe that the world can be changed through your own and other people's actions, the more likely it is you will participate in civic engagement. Values also play an important role in motivating people to engage civically and politically because values define what ought to be done. Scholars have identified some typical motivating values: concerns with injustice, definitions of democracy, conceptions of good citizenship, and so forth (Barrett and Pachi 2019: 38–41).

A weakness of these studies is evident: they add one more "cultural variable" to the already long list of independent variables, and the results often predictably follow the "civic culture" paradigm and rarely yield new findings beyond common sense. To remedy this issue, a study by Kraig Beyerlein and Stephen Vaisey switch the focus to the dependent variables (Beyerlein and Vaisey 2013). In other words, all civic actions are not the same: some are "bridging" – going beyond one's group to improve the broader society – while others are "bonding," enhancing internal solidarity without caring about the broader society. Then, Beyerlein and Vaisey ask, what moral worldviews matter in each type of civic action? Their findings revisit the enduring debates over individualism and religion and corroborate Wuthnow's argument that individualism is not incompatible with altruistic actions. But these researchers also have new findings. Compared to a worldview of civic responsibility, individualism less effectively encourages people to do "bridging" civic engagement. Compared to the idea that stresses one's duty for his or her faith-based community, it is also less useful in getting people involved in "bonding" engagement.

Another weakness of the "one-more-cultural-factor" approach is that individuals' agency in picking and choosing these values and beliefs is often downplayed. Values, beliefs, and attitudes that motivate civic engagement may vary across contexts and situations and are subject to the nexus of multiple factors (Erdurmazlı 2019). For example, volunteers at different life stages are motivated by different reasons: young novice volunteers are motivated for social reasons – earning credits for college and making friends – while older, regular volunteers are motivated for altruistic reasons (Compion et al. 2021).

The recent cultural sociological perspective attempts to correct this problem. For example, volunteering or civic engagement is reinterpreted as an action to seek one's *symbolic capital*, a term from Pierre Bourdieu, in the forms of social approval and moral recognition (Wilson and Musick 1997). In Bourdieu's theory, social actions can be viewed as processes of converting economic, social, and cultural capital to symbolic capital; in other words, people use various resources to seek social recognition and approval (Bourdieu and Wacquant 2013). Ten hours a week spent on volunteering might have worse economic returns than spending the ten hours on work or investment, but volunteering can be regarded as a reputable action and even an honor, a symbolic capital that work or investment may not be able to bring you. This recognition compels people to act.

Therefore, this theory can integrate many other studies. For example, one's income can be part of one's economic capital; the higher one's economic capital, the more likely one has the financial resources to participate in civic engagement and thus enhance one's symbolic capital – a better reputation through volunteering. A cynic may rightly point out that this is why many tycoons set up charitable foundations to contribute to public causes such as the environment and helping poor children – they want to gain public recognition or even whitewash their unsavory past by converting their economic capital to symbolic capital.

In this theory, what has been called "civic culture," including attitudes, knowledge, and preference, is *cultural capital*. Even though individuals are not always aware of it, their attitudes toward volunteer work and disposition to join public activities are part of the resources enabled and constrained by their social positions. In John Wilson and Marc Musick's study (Wilson and Musick 1997), religiosity is a key indicator of cultural capital about civic engagement. Churches are one of the common sources of the institutionalized culture of benevolence, and one's religiosity means the degree of exposure to such culture through formal activities and having more disposition and propensity to volunteer.

From a different perspective, Mary Alice Haddad argues that citizens' decision to volunteer or not, and what kinds of association they join, depend on not only individual-level factors but also the prevalent culture of civic responsibility in the community, "a general understanding among community residents of what an individual is expected to contribute to the community in order to be a citizen of good standing" (Haddad 2007: 28). In her study of Japanese volunteering, she shows that if the prevalent culture in a community is focused on the government's civic responsibility, then volunteering is often organized by "embedded organizations," such as volunteer fire departments, which rely on volunteers' labor but receive significant support from local governments. If the prevalent culture stresses that individual citizens should shoulder the responsibility for the welfare of the community, then volunteering is often organized by non-embedded organizations relatively independent of the government.

This cultural approach can explain the paradox that Japan has been generally perceived as a country with a "weak" civil society under a robust bureaucracy but, if examined closely, in fact has a vibrant civic life. The reason is that a large part of Japan's civic engagement is organized by embedded organizations in communities where the prevalent culture embraces governmental support and even demands that the government shoulder its civic responsibility. Outside observers with the preconception of an "independent civil society" usually look for a Japanese civil society in the wrong places. Even in contexts other than Japan, as I have discussed in chapter 3, the notion of unembedded civic engagement is a myth rather than reality.

Other studies emphasize the role of extreme situations, such as disasters, wars, and atrocities, in precipitating and activating civic engagement. Such situations generate social disruptions, cause death and human suffering, and highlight moral issues. Meanwhile, such situations also induce solidarity among people who have to go through the same difficulties (Collins 2004). This solidarity of pain usually motivates people to rush to the sites and offer their help. Kraig Beyerlein and David Sikkink use survey data to study what factors made 10 percent of adult Americans volunteer in one way or another after the 9/11 attacks (Beyerlein and Sikkink 2008). They found that solidarity was the key, but the solidarity had different levels. At the national level, the external attacks triggered a strong national solidarity, and thus Americans were eager to offer their help in the relief effort. Below the national level, individuals who participated in some kinds of community activities, such as candlelight vigils and community volunteering, tended to identify with the victims and were more likely to help. At the personal level, those who had personal identification with the victims, through personal networks with someone attacked or in danger, often volunteered because they felt a sense of responsibility to help.

The Art of Association: Effects of Civic Engagement

Tocqueville famously claims that institutions and associations for citizens to join together to pursue a common goal are *schools of democracy*, in which citizens learn, develop, and perfect the *art of association*. Although Tocqueville characteristically does not define its exact connotation, this "art of association" roughly means the civic skills of working with fellow citizens toward a common goal and democratic dispositions for tolerance, equality, freedom, and other key components in the culture of democracy (Tocqueville [1840] 2004: 599). In real-world civil societies, these effects of civic engagement widely exist but are often complicated and compromised by various situations, human natures, and dynamics of interactions.

Tolerance

A significant benefit of civic engagement, according to mainstream political theory, is developing an attitude of tolerance, an important element of the culture of democracy. This tolerance develops when people are exposed to and interact with different views and lifestyles. Such exposure and interaction make them understand the rationales of opposing views and thus reflect on their own views, and eventually lead to a reduction of group-based prejudice (Allport 1954). John Stuart Mill famously argues: "It is hardly possible to overstate the value ... of placing human beings in contact with other persons dissimilar to themselves, and with modes of thought and action unlike those with which they are familiar" (Mill 1848: 119).

In an influential empirical study, Diana C. Mutz uses survey and experiment data to confirm this general theory but with some important caveats (Mutz 2002). Mutz warns that exposure to different views does not automatically or directly lead to political tolerance. Rather, it is mediated by two mechanisms: first, the *cognitive mechanism*, one's "perspective-taking" ability, that is, one's ability to understand the rationales for opposing views. The more one is exposed to different views, the more likely one is to put oneself in others' shoes; consequently, mutual understanding leads to a higher degree of tolerance. Second, the *affective mechanism*, by which one's frequent interactions with others create intimacy, which reduces the hostility due to political differences. The more one interacts with people with different political views in activities not related to politics, the more one develops intimacy and affective relations, which reduce the animosity.

The two mechanisms Mutz tests in her study have important implications for democracy and civil society. The cognitive mechanism substantiates a greater willingness to extend civil liberties and freedom of speech to those groups one dislikes. It also emphasizes the significance of deliberation, by which, as I have discussed in chapter 2, people engage in reasonable discussions to find common ground and recognize differences. The affective mechanism interestingly suggests that apolitical interactions and avoiding politics in everyday interactions might be a good thing. You develop a friendship with someone in your running club and later find out that this person might support a presidential candidate you dislike. Both of you probably choose to ignore your different political opinions because you still want to run together three times a week.

Nevertheless, on many occasions, people tend *not* to talk and interact with people who are different from them. Rather, they tend to seek out like-minded people to form groups and have discussions about public issues. The colloquial saying "birds of a feather flock together" has been theoretically elaborated as the mechanism of *homophily*: people tend to develop networks and friendship with those who are like them (McPherson et al. 2001). Consequently, the more you engage in activities of associations, the more you interact with people who share your political views, lifestyles, and socioeconomic status. Civic engagement, therefore, reinforces what you believe instead of exposing you to different views. You may hide your bigotry toward a certain ethnic group when you interact with your fellow workers because you want to keep your job. But you find a "free-fire zone" in a tiny public that normalizes and even praises your bigotry. You seek to be comfortably ensconced in intolerance. Moreover, extremists tend to participate more because civic engagement provides them with opportunities to reap "expressive benefits," allowing them to openly express their ideologies that are not accepted in other social realms (Fiorina 1999).

Related to the homophily mechanism is a much-discussed issue, the *echo chamber effect* in online discussions. You think you are participating in discussions about public topics with various kinds of people, but you actually choose to listen to only what you feel is similar to your own opinions. Thus, you are not in a vast universe of ideas but a "chamber" in which you only hear your echo. Social media helps form this echo chamber. Online users choose which information they want to consume and thus avoid opposing views. Platforms use algorithms to automatically sort and even suggest information and products in line with our views. In the long run, as scholars and media commentators worry, such commercially constructed echo chambers lead to a fragmented, polarized public sphere. An even darker side of the echo chambers is that the lack of gatekeepers and abundance of bots in platforms tend to facilitate the spread of disinformation.

To break the echo chamber, online or offline, as many suggest, people need to be exposed to different and opposing views, to "talk across the aisle," so to speak. Such talks may make people move closer to the middle, become more moderate, and understand and recognize reasonable points from the other side. In fact, many formal deliberation programs described in chapter 3 are designed for such talk.

Cultural sociologists generally share this worry over the dark side of homophily but reveal some more complex mechanisms. As I have discussed in chapter 3, an association's goals and meanings matter for the association's internal solidarity and its contribution to society. Do the ends of associations also matter in nurturing their members' attitudes of tolerance? In other words, should we expect members of an anti-immigration group to demonstrate the same tolerance as members of an immigration rights group? Our common sense tells us we should not. Cultural sociologists agree.

They suggest a *cultural asymmetry* mechanism: people who self-selectively participate in associations with tolerance and diversity as core values tend to reinforce their tolerant attitudes in their interactions with different outsiders. For example, in a survey study of Belgians, Marc Hooghe finds that members of associations devoted to peace, human rights, the environment, and other topics with tolerance and diversity as explicit values tend to have a lower level of ethnocentrism in their practices (Hooghe 2003).

This cultural asymmetry argument also suggests that the echo chamber effect might be overestimated, at least among people who cherish the ideal of openness and tolerance. In a study of about 150 million tweets about political and nonpolitical issues, Pablo Barberá et al. find that liberals are significantly more likely to talk across the aisle, that is, more likely to retweet conservatives than conservatives are to retweet liberals (Barberá et al. 2015). Also, the polarization is less serious in discussions of less political topics, such as the 2014 Winter Olympics, than topics like the 2012 American presidential election.

Sociologist Chris Bail, however, discovers some different cultural mechanisms (Bail 2021). He asserts that social media should not take all the blame. Rather, the source of political polarization lies deep inside ourselves, in some of our basic social needs as humans: presenting different versions of ourselves, seeking recognition and status, and so on. But social media works like a "prism," which refracts those needs and provides us with a distorted understanding of ourselves and others. Thus, social media satisfies and even encourages extremists' desire to seek the status and recognition which they cannot achieve in real social life. They tend to go as extreme as possible to attract attention. The prevalence of extremists in online platforms mutes and deters moderates who find such dialogs unconstructive and even deleterious to them. Consequently, they lose interest in further participation and choose to exit. This, in turn, leaves social media discussions to extremists. A vicious cycle forms.

Bail's argument comes from two well-designed studies. In the first study, Bail and his colleagues created "bots," automatic Twitter accounts that retweeted the political messages of prominent liberals or conservatives (Bail 2021). Recruited research subjects received messages from bots, and the messages were from the subjects' opposite side, for example, a liberal-leaning research subject receiving messages from Breitbart News and a conservative from Nancy Pelosi. The subjects received $11 a day for following the bots, which sent twenty-four messages each day for one month. Before and after the experiment, the researchers measured the subjects' political views to see if the exposure to the opposing views led to any changes.

As it turned out, exposing the subjects to the views of the other side did not make them more moderate. Rather, it made Republicans significantly more conservative but did not make Democrats more liberal. This finding contradicts our received wisdom about "talking across the aisle" and cannot be easily explained by existing theories or the experimental data.

Bail then decided to use a more traditional method, in-depth interviews, to explain this phenomenon. The interviews revealed some underlying mechanisms that the bot experiment could not show. For example, enthusiastic partisans with extremist views, in contrast, found the attention they lacked in offline life, and the opposing views even strengthened their animosity and their political identity. Some of them became so-called "trolls," who feel recognized in the online culture of extremism.

For many moderates or unenthusiastic partisans, however, exposing themselves to opposite views made them feel uncomfortable. They "experience[d] stepping outside their echo chamber as an attack upon their identity" (Bail 2021: 31). Their moderate views may have encountered trolls' attacks. Or they may have been alienated from their families and friends who held different political views. They chose to leave or reduce their visits to the social media space to avoid animosity.

On the other hand, Bail opposes the idea that moderates should delete their Twitter accounts, because social media needs moderate people and reasonable discussions instead of becoming a playground for extremists. But how? Bail suggests several ways, for example, trying to put your ideas before your identity and avoiding using the polarizing leaders' opinions as a talking point.

Civic Skills

Civic skills, including the skills of participating in and organizing associational life, might be the most self-evident "art of association" effect of civic engagement. Many studies confirm this effect. For example, Irene Bloemraad and Veronica Terriquez found that community-based organizations in two low-income and semi-rural communities in California empowered individuals and nurtured their skills, such as making important decisions, giving public presentations, planning meetings and events, joining campaigns, collecting signatures, and so on (Bloemraad and Terriquez 2016).

Civic skills can also be transferred from one type of association to another. But such transfer depends on several factors, such as whether one is an active member of the association and how one is civically engaged. In a mixed-method study of Latino immigrant members of a labor union for janitors in Los Angeles, Terriquez shows that active union members felt empowered by their engagement in union activities and, consequently, participated more in the parents' activities in their children's schools (Terriquez 2011). In the words of one of the interviewees: "For somebody who didn't go to school for very long, the union is like a school" (2011: 595) For the active members of the union, this "school" taught them to speak up in public, raise demands, communicate with school decision-makers, and work with other parents to deal with the challenges their children faced in their schools. Note that most of the immigrants did not have a history of political participation in their home countries. In contrast, inactive union members also participated in school activities but their mindset was to "support" teachers and administrators, "do our part," do the assignments from the PTA, and ensure their kids did not have trouble in school, rather than engage themselves in activities that address schools' problems.

Do people learn the same art of association in mostly recreational, nonpolitical associations, for example, a bowling group or a chorus group? Putnam's answer is apparently "yes," but his answer largely hinges on a "social capital" assumption that more connections lead to more civic skills. Such an argument does not tell us much about whether the goals of an association matter. Tocqueville, in contrast, gives an unambiguous "no." When Tocqueville talks about associations as "free schools" for citizens to develop the art of association, in chapter 7 of volume II of *Democracy in America*, he emphasizes the importance of political association to civil associations: "Political associations can therefore be looked upon as vast free schools to which all citizens come to learn the general theory of association" ([1840] 2004: 606). It is possible for people to engage in small joint affairs in nonpolitical associations and learn the "art of association," which will eventually help political association. But a more important process is the other way around: "political association singularly develops and perfects civil associations" (Tocqueville [1840] 2004: 604). Therefore, in a country where political association is prohibited, "civil associations will always be few in number, weak in conception, and lacking in leadership and will either refuse to entertain ambitious projects or fail in executing them" ([1840] 2004: 607).

From another perspective, the civic skills participating citizens develop are not just a result of individual efforts; rather, how they develop those skills depends on how the association defines the participants' roles and identities. In a study of how two nonprofit organizations turn their members into active and competent citizens, Jennifer Dodge and Sonia M. Ospina show that the organizations attributed the local chemical plant problems to the state's responsibility instead of viewing it as an isolated issue. Thus, the members were defined as citizens who were responsible for speaking up about the issues instead of consumers who purchased services from the organizations and participated through providing feedback (Dodge and Ospina 2016).

Many other scholars, however, convey a less optimistic message: acquiring civic skills does not always mean the participants develop democratic dispositions, such as tolerance and equality. There could be opposite effects. Ariel C. Armony's study of Argentina's citizens who participate in nonprofit organizations shows these mixed effects (Armony 2004). While the participants learned civic skills through their participation and used the skills in other areas, they often openly expressed their ethnicity- and class-based discriminations, making derogatory remarks about Jews, *"negros"* (the "dark-skinned"), *"villeros"* (shantytown inhabitants), and the other poor. One of the participants even openly said in a group discussion, "I am not ashamed of revealing that I'm a racist." Such a remark was not met with challenges. These expressions were in stark contrast with the goals of the associations: devotion to human rights and civil rights issues. In addition, a fair amount of cynicism and lack of trust were also evident among the participants. An explanation for this lack of democratic disposition is that the associations can only be as good as their environments. They embodied many prevailing vices in Argentine society after democratization, such as distrust of the corrupt political institutions and rampant racism.

Even in the associational life where explicit class and ethnic discriminations are absent, the learning of civic skills, as scholars point out, is highly stratified and skewed toward the more privileged (Verba et al. 1995). Such skewing, however, is less a result of civic engagement per se than of stratified preparedness for civic engagement: middle- and higher-class citizens already learn more civic skills than lower- and working-class people, such as speaking, writing, and organizing, through education and work. Again, associations can only be as good as their environments. Civic engagement works like a process of "reproduction" of cultural capital. A study by Philip Schwadel showed that local churches, which were believed to be less stratified than most associations, served as the basis for higher-income members to receive most civic skill practices and training. Although the lower-income members also participated in charity, public policy, or social justice organizations within their churches, they were less likely to participate in decision-making on finance and administration (Schwadel 2002).

Apathy and Hope

It is not uncommon that once civically engaged people see other people's suffering, they ask, "What causes the suffering?" The answer often has to do with problems of malpractice, flaws in institutions, and abuses of power. Then a dilemma is presented to them: do you want to take a step further to address the causes or just turn around and leave? Ideally, civic engagement, by definition, should naturally and eventually lead to a collective effort to solve social problems and cure moral vices to make the society a better place, in accordance with one's image of a good society. People who participate in voluntary associations are more likely than nonparticipants to join in political activities, such as protests, voting, and other collective actions (Theiss-Morse and Hibbing 2005: 238).

Nevertheless, many participants in civic engagement do not take this step. The factors that prevent them from addressing the causes of suffering are many. In chapter 3, I have presented Eliasoph's research findings that avoiding politics results from *speech norms* within grassroots associations (Eliasoph 1998). In another study, Eliasoph identifies the same phenomenon but finds a slightly different mechanism: civil associations like the youth empowerment program she studied develop an organizational style that leads the volunteers further away from addressing the causes (Eliasoph 2011). This does not mean that organizers of associations do not care about the suffering of the people. On the contrary, they do; they also want the youth participants to know "how other people actually live" – sometimes distant suffering indeed, the people living in a place far away from theirs – and use "no-brainer" ways to help out, like "Candies for Kosovo" or collecting cans of tuna for the hungry. They are "no-brainers" because they produce obvious goodness: smiles on children's faces, cans of tuna possibly consumed by the needy, candies possibly received by kids in Kosovo, and so on.

Do those activities have real effects? Such programs may have very few effects on the participants' willingness or preparedness for engaging in activities to solve the problems. Eliasoph poignantly says: "The can of tuna did not help volunteers learn about local lives. Collecting the can of tuna put youth volunteers closer to the can of tuna" (2011: 92). Similarly, in an ethnographic study of the Mobile Soup Kitchen (MSK), a program that distributes free food among the homeless, Aaron Horvath shows that although MSK volunteers feel satisfied in their meaningful interactions with the homeless, their preconceptions about the homeless and themselves remain unchanged (Horvath 2020). Seeing themselves more as observers of the homeless community, they still feel uneasy, unprepared to deal with the problems they witness, and with no faith in alternative solutions, such as government programs and other political solutions.

Some scholars, however, may not see this political apathy as pathology. Hibbing and Theiss-Morse argue that most people under democracy, at least Americans, prefer "stealth democracy" – "stealth" meaning invisible, as in "stealth aircraft"(Hibbing and Theiss-Morse 2002). They neither want to know too much about politics nor are willing to participate in decision-making processes, although they do want to know that such ways of participation are available for them to hold the government accountable in unusual situations. Therefore, what is believed to be "political apathy" is a normal state. It is pointless to worry about it; it is even unrealistic to mobilize everyone to participate in politics. In other words, "couch potatoes" who are more interested in Netflix than attending civic group meetings are not an existential threat to democracy.

This argument is based on the notion that democracy means an electoral system and politics is a highly specialized profession. In contrast, most scholars of civil society presume that democracy means a democratic social life, a broader concept than the representative system. Moreover, the subjects of the studies discussed above are civically engaged people, active minorities compared to the general population. They are willing to devote their time and money to causes that they believe will make the society better. Thus, it is reasonable to expect these active people to discuss and take action on the problems they witness. The fact that they do not do so speaks volumes about the problems in civil society.

Some scholars take a different perspective and see some positive things in this avoidance. They urge us not to take people's claim "I'm not political" at face value. The claim, as Elizabeth A. Bennett et al. show (Bennett et al. 2013), could be just a rhetorical device for active participants to distance themselves from "ugly politics" – the self-interested, conflictual, and corrupt politics of the conventional image. Therefore, participants who disavow politics do not stop working; rather, they cherish a positive civic imagination to envision a better society, which inspires their engagement. Bennett et al.'s finding differs from Eliasoph's "avoiding politics" on a subtle point. Eliasoph's participants *actually* avoid politics and narrow their circle of concerns to local, fixable things without trying to go beyond their apolitical zone. Bennett et al.'s participants only *rhetorically* avoid politics but broaden their scope and continue to take part in activities to remedy issues. In sum, the apolitical claim is a way to interpret and justify their civic engagement.

For many active participants, however, such apathy is more a result of restrictions in the political context than of their unwillingness to get involved. In some situations, volunteers witness problems that are too blatant for them to ignore, but addressing the causes of those problems may have negative effects on their career and life. Such situations can occur anywhere, under any political system, but it is under a repressive, authoritarian regime that this political-moral dilemma is insoluble for civically engaged citizens. In those contexts, democracy is not "stealth" but "absent."

The Sichuan earthquake volunteers in my research are those who tried to deal with this dilemma (Xu 2017). Many volunteers had the experience of teaching in a tent school. Not far from their tent was a pile of ruins, which the volunteers passed on a daily basis. This pile of ruins might entomb 100 or 200 students. Altogether 5,335 students died in their schools, according to official statistics. The official media explained the collapse of schools as a result of the earthquake. But very few volunteers really believed this explanation, because many of them saw rebars in the ruins as thin as chopsticks, concrete mixed with large amounts of sand, and sometimes no rebars or concrete at all. They also heard stories of, and even saw first-hand, how the students' bodies were dug out of the rubble, dead and rotten. They felt the unspeakable trauma of the parents. All these experiences would have naturally led many volunteers to a simple question: "Why did so many schools collapse?" They also wondered: "I volunteered because

I wanted to reduce the people's suffering, but should I cross the boundary to address the causes of their suffering, through serious and open public deliberations, and even activism to find out causes of the suffering?"

Those who answered "yes" joined the campaigns launched by activists Ai Weiwei and Tan Zuoren to collect and verify the names of student victims. These campaigners were harassed, pursued, threatened, expelled, and detained by the government. Tan Zuoren was sentenced to five years in prison. Those who answered "no" were safe but felt a sense of guilt that kept gnawing at their conscience. It was one thing to make angry comments online as a distant netizen; it was quite another if one actually went there, talked with the embittered survivors, and had to directly face this dilemma. Volunteers used all kinds of rhetorical devices to get around the difficult questions they faced daily, telling themselves: "It's normal in this society" or "I can't change anything, and so I'll forget about it" or simply "I don't care." Their apathy was a result of both an actual threat from the authorities and, probably more common, a fear of imminent threat implied in the political context – the "chilling effect." That was what most Sichuan volunteers and volunteers under repressive regimes in general chose to do.

Nevertheless, this chapter should end on a more positive note: despite all the problems and challenges, civic engagement does bring hope to disadvantaged groups who previously lacked accesses to public and political life. More specifically, this "hope" contains cultural and political imaginings about those groups' possibility and ability to improve the societies. An even more positive note is that such hope occurs in some unexpected places. In 2003, women won thirty-nine seats in the eighty-member Chamber of Deputies in Rwanda, the country's lower house of legislature. This unusual victory for women made Rwanda the country with the highest percentage of female in its legislature, followed by Sweden (Burnet 2008). This progressive outcome not only occurred just less than a decade after the country suffered from one of the most horrendous genocides in human history (see chapter 6) but also happened under an increasingly authoritarian state. In chapter 5, I will discuss in detail the complex relationships between the civil society groups for women and the Rwandan Patriotic Front that controlled the state. The reader certainly should not expect a rosy picture. But suffice it to say here that the strong presence of women in the legislature greatly shaped the "collective cultural imagination" of gender in Rwanda society (Burnet 2008: 382). It transformed self-perceptions and public perceptions about women's role from secondary, subordinate "daughters and wives" to active and vocal participants in civic life, even assuming leadership positions. This transformation, as researchers believe, will pave the way for Rwandan women to participate in a more democratic political system in the future (Burnet 2008: 386).

5

The Culture of Democracy Under Undemocratic States

According to *The Economist*'s Democracy Index 2020, only seventy-five countries (44.9 percent) are "full" or "flawed" democracies. The United States is tellingly labelled a "flawed democracy;" so is France. Thirty-five countries (21.0 percent) have "hybrid" regimes that contain significant undemocratic components, and fifty-seven (34.1 percent) exhibit outright "authoritarianism," an increase from fifty-three in 2019. In other words, more than half of the states in the world are more or less undemocratic (The Economist Intelligence Unit 2021).

We obviously cannot afford to neglect civil societies in more than half of the countries in the world. Nevertheless, we also should not follow a prevailing misconception in public discourses that a "real" civil society must stand up against the undemocratic state, like the famous icon "tank man" standing in front of an array of the Chinese military's tanks in the 1989 Tiananmen incident. Or that civil societies should at least be financially and institutionally independent of the undemocratic state. If they are not, this reasoning goes, then they are not bona fide civil societies.

This normative concept of "civil society" has its empirical foundation. When "civil society" was revived in the late twentieth century, particularly under Communism in Central and Eastern Europe in the 1970s and 1980s (Arato 1981), it was a rallying cry of the self-organized activists, a term to describe the relatively independent social space they carved out and the ideal society they longed to build. It was used as a slogan and a buzzword for academics, the media, and organizations to understand and motivate activities leading to democratization. It has shown the power of an idea through the reactions of its enemy. Undemocratic regimes are perturbed about the potential political dangers that civil society may pose to them and even censor the term "civil society."

Cultural sociology takes the normative implication of "civil society" seriously but empirically regards it as part of the reality of actual civil societies. Cultural sociology examines how this normative idea has inspired, informed, and motivated people to engage in public activities under undemocratic states. Cultural sociology also recognizes the fact that not all, not even the majority, of the associations in undemocratic contexts stand in front of tanks. Rather, to survive in harsh environments, many conform to the official political cultures, while others compromise by changing language to seek common ground with undemocratic states. Numerous associations and individuals remain carefully apolitical. This *complex coexistence* of civil societies and undemocratic states goes beyond the simplistic pattern of "civil society versus the state." Recent crises of civil societies in places like Hong Kong and elsewhere show how precarious such complex coexistence is under a robust and ruthless authoritarian regime.

The Culture of Democracy Under Communism in Central and Eastern Europe

The concept of "civil society" revived as an interpretation and justification of the collective effort to achieve democracy under Communism in Central and Eastern European countries, especially in Poland, in the 1970s and 1980s. The "democracy" that the activists pursued was initially a *democratic social life*, which was ironically phrased as "anti-politics." Rather than directly challenging the states, the effort aimed to "empower citizens, to arouse in people a sense of their own value, their worth, their dignity as humans and as citizens" in an autonomous social space (Ost 1990: 4). The term "anti-politics" did not mean apolitical or apathetic. Under a repressive, Leninist state that attempted to impose total control over social life, any pursuit of independent social life was an effort to achieve some unusual changes – not from the top down but from the bottom up. It was this notion of *independence* that later discourses of "civil society" emphasized. This emphasis, however, should not overshadow other important notions in the culture of democracy in Central and Eastern European civil society, that is, *equality* and *solidarity* across the intellectual/worker and secular/religious divides.

Civil society in Poland in the 1960s to 1980s was a good example. The culture of democracy in Polish civil society grew in the "revisionism" period, in which the Polish state, under the leadership of Władysław Gomułka, attempted to distance itself from the Soviet Union, to revive the tradition of social democracy within Communism, and to pursue the relaxation of society and culture. As Adam Michnik, a prominent Polish intellectual, aptly pointed out, the revisionists were unfaithful to the church (the USSR) but faithful to the scripture (Marxism) (Bernhard 1993). Unlike Alexander Dubček in Czechoslovakia, who pursued an open agenda of liberalization in the "Prague Spring," Gomułka vacillated between relaxation and restriction. Throughout the Gomułka period, civil society as a sphere of associations and discourses gradually developed. The University of Warsaw retained most of its intellectual freedom, and intellectuals' circles, such as the "Crooked Circle Club," became active (Kennedy 1991: 28). Nevertheless, social democracy was only the state's "coquettish ideology," which "was meant to seduce a renascent civil society" to help the Party (Ost 1990: 41). As Gomułka's repressive side became evident, the intellectuals and others in the budding civil society were disillusioned.

In January 1968, a seemingly insignificant incident changed the dynamics of state–society interactions. Adam Mickiewicz's *Forefathers' Eve*, a classic Polish drama, was put on for propaganda purposes, but some anti-Czarist-Russian lines in the show, like "Everyone sent here from Moscow is either a jackass, a fool, or a spy" (Kennedy 1991: 32), received subversive interpretations that alluded to the Soviet control over Poland. After a show, about

300 members of the audience marched out of the theatre and started a protest gathering (Kemp-Welch 2008: 148). The show was soon banned, but Warsaw University students continued their protests. A crackdown came. Students were beaten; professors fired; departments dissolved. The regime also used the protest as a pretext to launch an anti-Semitic campaign to persecute students and officials of Jewish descent. This incident marked the end of revisionism.

When Polish intellectuals reflected on the failure of revisionism, they reached the conclusion that placing their hope in a leader was wrong. A bottom-up change instead of a top-down reform should be the goal of future pursuits. For example, in his famous essay "Theses on Hope and Hopelessness," Leszek Kołakowski described the "hopelessness" of struggles under state socialism: the state monopolized the economy and politics; state officials were politically servile people rather than experts; the state used misinformation as a ruling mechanism and had a natural tendency to destroy all independent forms of social life, and so on. Yet there was hope. State socialism could not solve several contradictory internal tendencies, such as the conflict among factions and sectors within the state and the bankruptcy of the official ideology (Ost 1990: 58–64). To take advantage of the contradictions, Kołakowski argues, an independent civil society must exist to achieve *societal democratization* instead of persuading the state to reform itself.

Two other influential Polish intellectuals, Adam Michnik and Jacek Kuroń, made similar points about the possibility of a democratic social life. "The strategy of the opposition, therefore, should be to reconstruct social ties. *The social is the political*" (Ost 1990: 66). If people engaged in any social activity that the party-state could not control – even a sports team – they were part of the opposition insofar as they were counteracting the totalitarian tendency of the system. This argument sounded like a mirror-image version of Putnam's "bowling alone" thesis – nonpolitical, self-organizing activities also have functions for democracy – only it was long before Putnam and aimed to resist the Communist state rather than buttressing a consolidated democracy.

This idea was also prevalent among intellectuals in other Soviet-bloc countries. For example, Václav Havel in Czechoslovakia advocated for a "parallel structure" which grew from "the aims of life and the authentic needs of real people" rather than the system and abstract theories. In this space, people "live within the truth" even amid systemic lies. All eventual changes in the system should come about from below rather than from above (Havel 1985: 79–80). In such a parallel structure,

> The spectrum of its expressions and activities is naturally very wide. It includes everything from self-education and thinking about the world, through free creative activity and its communication to others, to the most varied free, civic attitudes, including instances of independent social self-organization. In short, it is an area in which living within the truth becomes articulate and materializes in a visible way. (Havel 1985: 65)

In sum, by the mid-1970s, Central and Eastern European intellectuals had already articulated a *culture of democracy* centered on the idea of "liberty," which was interpreted as independence from the repressive regimes.

Another element of the culture of democracy was the solidarity between intellectuals and workers. In the second half of the 1970s, Polish intellectuals started associations like KOR (Komitet Obrony Robotników, the Workers' Defense Committee) to provide legal, medical, and financial assistance for those workers repressed by the party-state in the 1976 strike (Kemp-Welch 2008).

KOR was a historically significant step in the development of Polish civil society. It was not a salon for intellectuals. Instead, it was an association for intellectuals to venture out of their comfort zone and realize their ideas of self-governing space and change from below in organizational unity with workers. In this sense, KOR and similar organizations would be Tocqueville's favorites. They performed the function of what he termed "free schools," which taught both the intellectuals and the workers the "art of association" (Tocqueville [1840] 2004: 599). The intellectuals' "habits of the heart" were enlarged to include not only liberty, their original idea, but also some elements of *equality* and *solidarity* – united with workers and treating them as equals.

KOR aimed to achieve several specific goals: to end the state's reprisals against the worker strikers; to provide the strikers with legal assistance; to demand amnesty for those imprisoned; to rehabilitate the strikers in their former positions; to provide an account of the state's repression in 1976; and to bring to justice officials responsible for the abuse of the law and the use of torture (Bernhard 1993: 101). As expected, these activities provoked the state's repression: KOR was declared an illegal organization in November 1976. The police raided a KOR meeting and detained members. The crackdown provoked protests from KOR and other groups of intellectuals and workers, which culminated in May 1977 when a student and KOR activist was found dead. KOR and other groups held a week-long strike, and their efforts were implicitly endorsed by the Catholic Church and received much international support. The state finally acceded to the mounting grievances and released the KOR detainees and workers in July.

A particularly important move after the amnesty struggle was the KOR's newspaper *Robotnik* (The Worker), which started in 1977 as a public forum for the workers to "publish their independent opinions, exchange experiences, and make contacts with workers at other factories" (Bernhard 1993: 160). Its stated goals included to defend workers' interests, expand workers' participation on the questions of pay, working and living conditions, and support independent workers' unions. The newspapers were distributed in factories, shipyards, and churches in major industrial cities in Poland. *Robotnik* was more than just a newspaper; rather, it connected workers from different places, published guidelines for conducting strikes, and served as a mechanism of coordinating collective action – for example, it produced the Charter of Workers' Rights, signed by 100 activists, including skilled workers and intellectuals, as well as engineers and technicians.

Another invention in the Polish civil society was the "flying universities," underground academies where political dissidents and intellectuals offered classes about the country's history, culture, and politics (Getler 1978). The flying universities usually gathered in private houses and moved from place to place, which was the origin of the name. Famous intellectuals and dissidents, including Michnik and Kuroń, taught in the flying universities. Their explicitly stated purpose was not political but academic – to educate citizens and look for truth. Prestigious academic intellectuals endorsed this "pure academic" claim, publicly formed the "Society for Academic Courses" to support the flying universities, and agreed to give lectures. The state attempted to harass the professors and students. They were sometimes intercepted and arrested by the Polish government on their way to classes. Classes were sometimes disrupted, and students were pressured not to attend. But the flying universities were never completely shut down or suppressed. They survived in small spaces, in fluid and mobile forms, under the repressive regime.

A particularly important component of the culture of democracy in the Polish civil society was Catholicism. The Polish Catholic Church was both a relatively independent social institution and an incarnation of moral authority and national identity. Because of the sheer size of the church – the majority of Poles were Catholics – the Communist regime could not eliminate it but had to allow its existence. To some extent, the church had already carved out a relatively autonomous social space before it collaborated with the associations of intellectuals and workers. At several critical junctures, the church implicitly or explicitly supported them. For example, in the 1976 strike, the church and its bishops unequivocally protested the persecution of the worker strikers.

More important was the role of the Catholic Church in sustaining the culture of democracy, being "a creator, repository, and propagator of national, civic, and ethical values to a degree rarely found in other national churches" (Kubik 1994: 119). In the Polish Catholic Church's discourse, an ideal society should be free and respectful of human rights. In this ideal society, the Catholic Church must be independent of the state: "render to Caesar the things that are Caesar's, and to God the things that are God's." Leaders of the church expressed their unambiguous adherence to democratic ideals and presented the church as the champion of human rights. For example, Stefan Wyszyński, the cardinal of Poland, said in one of his Holy Cross Sermons:

> The courageous defense of freedoms and of the right to unite or organize for one's aims is therefore absolutely necessary, as well as the freedom of the press, public opinion, publication, discussion, deliberation, and scientific research. These are the prerequisites for creating the wealth of cultural, social, national, and political life. (Kubik 1994: 123)

Equally important was the Catholic Church's essential role as a depository of national identity: being a Pole meant being a Catholic, and vice versa. Freedom from Communism meant solidarity and equality among Catholic Poles. In this cultural imagining, liberty, equality, and solidarity were organically combined in this faith-based, national community.

The cultural expressions of Catholicism culminated in Pope John Paul II's historic visit to Poland, his homeland, in 1979. The visit was described as a "psychological earthquake" or "second baptism" for Poland (Kubik 1994). About a million believers attended the first mass in Warsaw, which was also televised throughout the country. Hundreds of thousands took on pilgrimages to attend other masses. The huge crowds were well controlled and orderly, organized not by the state but by the Poles themselves, who demonstrated their remarkable discipline and courtesy.

More important than the crowds were the pope's words and their long-lasting effects on the mentality of the Poles. In his sermons, Pope John Paul II called for dignity, respect for man, truth, justice, law, and tolerance. He personified the church and the nation and gave faith-based meanings to the lifeworld of Poland, and Communism therefore even looked more like a meaningless, foreign power imposed on the nation (Kennedy 1991: 44). *Robotnik*'s editorials also enthusiastically endorsed and welcomed his visit and the resulting reinvigoration of Polish Catholicism.

The development of Polish Catholicism, as Kennedy rightly argues, was a cultural prelude to Solidarność. Catholicism provided the developing civil society and the movement with a self-identification, an emancipatory vocabulary, and a model for self-organization (Kennedy 1991: 364). Most intellectuals and workers were Catholic. In workers' demonstrations, a juxtaposition of banners celebrating oppositional solidarity and religious piety was ubiquitous: "Long live the Polish United Workers' Party!" with "Mother of God be always with us" (Kubik 1994: 104).

In sum, in Polish civil society in the 1970s, intellectuals, workers, and Catholics, despite their different cultural and political agendas, shared the same set of political ideas revolving around freedom from state tyranny, equality among people with different class backgrounds, and solidarity of the faith-based national community. The ideas were realized in self-organizing practices and organizations like KOR. Thus, the opposition did not directly intend to overthrow the state but told the state to "let me be, leave me alone, don't try to tell me how to live" (Keane 1988: 5). Consequently, the synergy of ideas and practices, intellectuals and workers, religious and secular people, led to the success of Solidarność.

Civil Society and Democratization

Poland's civil society story, however, was idiosyncratic. Scholars have pointed out that "apart from Poland, there is no convincing evidence that organized civil society contributed to the communist collapse" (Ekiert and Kubik 2014: 55). Even in Poland, the decisive stage of democratic transition happened when the "anti-political politics" eventually became realpolitik, through strikes, negotiations, and elections. Nevertheless, as the Polish story diffused around the world, it was simplified into a myth of "civil society." With proactive, courageous "civil society" actors as the main characters, the story's happy ending was the success of Solidarność, the fall of Communism, and the establishment of a representative democratic system. All these were achieved without bloodshed. Some important historical and cultural specificities were dropped from the myth (Keane 1988).

This story was linear and simplistic, but it was exactly its simplicity that made the hype for "civil society." Together with other cases in the "third wave of democratization" (Huntington 1991), the Polish story offered a recipe for foundations, international organizations, think tanks, government agencies, and various political forces: to pursue democracy and enhance governance in undemocratic contexts, we need to support civil societies there. It justified billions of dollars flowing from funders in liberal democracies to the grassroots associations struggling under undemocratic regimes. Correspondingly, it also agitated those undemocratic regimes to closely monitor and meticulously restrict civil associations' activities. Both the civil society and the undemocratic state had the Polish story in their minds: one hoped to replicate it, and the other was worried about its replication. For instance, almost immediately after Solidarność's agreement with the Polish government in 1980, some high-ranking officials in the Chinese Communist Party (CCP) were alerted to the possibility that a similar oppositional organization could occur in China. This worry eventually reversed some leaders' earlier attempts to reform the political system in a more liberal direction (Wu 2014).

This myth of civil society was also what the right in the West in the 1980s were waiting for. They attacked state regulations under both Communism and the "free world." They enthusiastically embraced and promoted laissez-faire capitalism. The irony was that the right were endorsed by power from above, the *states* that followed Reaganism–Thatcherism, rather than from below. This political trend was also manifested in the conservative interpretation of Tocqueville, which highlighted localism, criticized administrative centralization, and cheered for American democracy in its global triumph over Communism (Schleifer 2012: 163–4). Against this background, the Polish story converged with "neo-Tocquevillianism" (Putnam 2000). The myth of "civil society" began to have a life of its own.

This myth was responsible for the considerable ink wasted on questions like whether civil society inevitably leads to democracy. To many scholars of democratization, the "dependent variable" of this question may be a bit too simplistic because democratization is often complex, prolonged, and nonlinear. Not all democratization will lead to full, consolidated democracy (Haerpfer et al.

2019). Rather, democratization may zigzag through twists and turns. It often leads to short-lived democracy, electoral autocracy, and other "hybrid" regimes; even if it is accomplished, it can slide back into an undemocratic regime.

Moreover, this myth and the corresponding debate exclusively focus on representative democracy as the outcome but neglect that a democratic social life may develop and even flourish under an undemocratic regime. This kind of democratic cultural change may be seen as the preparation stage for formal democratization. In fact, Polish civil society before the Solidarność movement was such a case. Whether the democratic social life will lead to regime transition depends on other conditions, such as economic, military, and social crises, and the synergy of other agents. Civil society alone cannot accomplish this grand mission. Cultural sociology, thus, urges us to expand our scope to understand the changing culture of democracy throughout the whole democratization process.

This perspective sheds new light on some successful cases of democratization. South Korea's democratization, which lasted for three decades and experienced several stages (1960s to 1980s), was guided by a more explicitly stated political goal of democratization than the "anti-political politics" in Poland (Kim 2000). Such a culture of democracy took the form of a dichotomy – civil society versus the authoritarian state, democracy versus dictatorship, and so on – which was realized "during the direct, intense, and sometimes brutal confrontation between civil society and the state" (Kim 2000: 147). Part of the reason for this explicitly political feature was that the authoritarian Korean state maintained some elements of a democratic facade, such as an election system. The election was certainly flawed and rigged, but its democratic pretension generated unintended consequences, especially citizens' awareness of democracy and political participation. In 1971, opposition candidate Kim Dae-jung won about 45 percent of the vote against Park Chung-hee, who had just removed the term limit for presidency and sought his third term and potentially lifelong terms. Park felt threatened by Kim's popular support and quickly introduced the Yushin Constitution, which gave him de facto dictatorial power. As Park took off his pseudo-democratic mask, civil society groups, including students, workers, and the Protestant and Catholic Churches, escalated their anti-dictatorship movement, which culminated in the Gwangju Uprising in 1980. The final round of democratization (1984–7) started when the overconfident Chun Doo-hwan regime relaxed its grip on civil society. Civil society groups seized the opportunity and organized into a tightly united national movement which contributed to the final transition. As scholar Sunhyuk Kim argues, however, this confrontational culture of democracy, especially in an intense political context, amplified radicalism and dichotomous thinking, and somewhat hindered the development of its nonconfrontational side, such as negotiation, deliberation, and compromise (Kim 2000: 147).

In other contexts, the culture of democracy suffered from its deficiency and failed to carve out a social space with democratic social life, let alone a direct challenge to the repressive state. For example, in the 1980s, many scholars and commentators expected that the burgeoning civil society in China in the 1980s would lead to potential democratization. Such expectations seemed plausible during the 1989 Tiananmen protest. But the 1989 movement only revealed some critical weaknesses in the culture of democracy in Chinese civil society.

First, most major figures in the Chinese civil society preferred a top-down strategy – to influence leaders to promote their agenda, an approach similar to the "revisionism" before the bottom-up, "anti-political" politics of the Polish civil society.

Second, the culture of democracy in the Chinese civil society in the 1980s lacked explicit expressions about equality and solidarity, two crucial values in the Polish civil society, as well as practices to realize such values (Calhoun 1994: 188–212). In the 1980s, there was no organization like KOR in China. The Chinese intellectuals had no intention to build serious alliances with the workers (Walder and Gong 1993). They identified themselves with the traditional elite literati, who shouldered the responsibility for the nation rather than integrating themselves with the working class. Some intellectuals even insisted on the need to restrict public discourse to those with the appropriate educational background (Calhoun 1994: 91).

Third, unlike in Poland, nationalism was on the side of the Chinese Communist Party. The Party depicted itself as a guardian and savior of the Chinese nation against foreign – Western, Japanese, and later Soviet – imperialism. Finally, China's Catholic Church – or any religion – did not play the significant role of the Polish church in fostering a culture of democracy. The Chinese Catholic Church was weak both culturally and organizationally. More importantly, due to the state's intervention and manipulation, the Chinese Catholic Church practiced the opposite of the culture of democracy: the priority of vertical rather than horizontal relationships, mutual mistrust and even belligerence, sectional loyalty and interests, and lack of "civic morality," represented in "the virtues of civility: self-restraint, tolerance for diversity, and a commitment to fair treatment for all" (Madsen 1998: 14).

Another angle from which to examine the complexity in the relationship between civil society and democratization is to see how civil society works in the process of consolidation of democracy, the final stage of democratization. Poland again provides a classic case, which, however, was less upbeat for civil society enthusiasts. After the successful Round Table negotiation, the leading figures in the Polish civil society, intellectuals and Solidarność leaders, turned themselves into staunch supporters and practitioners of the Balcerowicz Plan, a "shock therapy" policy of radical marketization and privatization. The workers, the heroes of the democratization, were stunned by their unemployment and pay cuts after democracy was established. The dream they had been fighting for became a nightmare. The intellectuals and the leaders of Solidarność tried to explain to the angry workers that their pain was inevitable and that the stupefying marketization was the best available option, from which they would eventually benefit. The persuasion failed. Workers launched strikes again but this time against the union leaders who once were workers like them and the intellectuals who had printed newsletters for them. Then the enraged workers were viewed as a problem, and marketization was believed in as the ultimate solution. Support for Solidarność plunged, as the workers turned to right-wing, religious nationalism. The exemplary "civil society" transformed itself into its enemy (Ost 2005).

This shocking transformation, however, is not incomprehensible from the perspective of the culture of democracy. Although the intellectuals and worker elites emphasized solidarity, communication, and openness in their civil society practices, the central element of their culture of democracy was liberty, which, in that context, was interpreted as independence from the Communist regime. After the Round Table negotiation, the drawback of this anti-state emphasis became evident. The culture of democracy that once guided the democratization now deteriorated into a neoliberal agenda. The market was regarded as the strongest force to dismantle the remainders of the old regime, whereas other elements in the culture of democracy, especially equality and solidarity, were soon abandoned. The "civil society against the state" pattern was further simplified into "us" versus "them." If you don't side with "us," the anti-Communist camp, including the opposition and the market, then you side with dead Communism. Hence, the culture of democracy in the Polish civil society soon invited the market in through the back door.

Post-World War II Japan, in contrast, provides a case in which new institutional structures and culture of democracy merge with traditional practices and values and produce new cultural foundation for democratic consolidation (Haddad 2012). Japan's contemporary democracy was imposed by the American Occupation on the country after the war. This unusual democratization process has led to a consolidated, healthy democracy (in the aforementioned Democracy Index 2020 by *The Economist*, Japan has quietly moved from "flawed democracy" to "full democracy," higher than some major Western countries, including France, the United States, and Italy). A distinctive but often neglected foundation for Japan's consolidation is the civil society development and corresponding democratic values that emphasize inclusiveness and respect through incorporating traditional practices and values into civil society organizations and engagement.

This merging of the old and the new was manifested in a distinctive form of association in Japanese civil society: traditional, community-based organizations. But their history was unsavory. When Japan militarism rose in the first half of the twentieth century, those traditional organizations played a crucial role in helping the state in war mobilization and total control over society. After being abolished during the American Occupation period, the traditional organizations revived to provide associational life for local neighborhoods, women, youth, and elderlies, and to offer social services. But these are not replicas of the old organizations. Rather, they adjust to the new democratic context by diversifying their membership and reducing the hierarchical authority structure within themselves. This change certainly did not happen overnight but through long-term societal transformation and generational shifts in political culture. As a chief of a neighborhood association describes: "The neighborhood associations democratized at the same time as society; they both did it together" (Haddad 2012: 113). On the other hand, the traditional emphasis on individuals' relations to each other and thus the importance of community persists in those associations and integrates effectively into the communitarian culture of the civil society.

Complex Coexistence: Civil Societies Under Contemporary Undemocratic Regimes

With very few exceptions such as North Korea, under contemporary undemocratic states, civil societies still exist (Lewis 2013). They are engaged in complex interactions with the undemocratic states. Opposition and contestation are certainly an important form of such interactions, but many, if not most, associations and individuals do not directly challenge states. In sum, there is a *complex coexistence* between civil societies and undemocratic states (Xu 2017).

This complex coexistence results from the undemocratic states' ambivalence toward civil societies. On the one hand, the states need civil associations to provide critical social services and perform important functions, and this need generates some room for civil societies. On the other hand, the states are vigilant for the associations' potential political risks and restrict their activities, especially those associations with explicitly stated political purposes. Within the political boundaries, associations and individuals can conduct their activities and express their opinions with varying degrees of freedom.

In the sections that follow, I lay out four different ways in which associations and individuals in civil societies express their ideas and meanings about their participation in civil society when they are interacting with the authoritarian state (see table 5.1): *opposition and contestation*; *compromise and negotiation*; *conformity and adherence*; *silence and avoidance*. Note that these four different ways are analytical distinctions. Different civil associations may coexist with the state in different ways (Cavatorta 2013). Even the same association may be in different relations with the state at different times: it might openly challenge the state at one point but negotiate with the state according to its judgment of the situation at another moment.

Opposition and Contestation

Associations and individuals sometimes openly challenge undemocratic states' official ideology or policies, uphold the ideal of democracy and human rights, and thus are subject to the states' harassment and suppression. Many such oppositional associations are active in the countries where the undemocratic states have a weaker ability to control the society and/or there is a partial or nominal election system, although a few may also exist under strong states. Typical examples are human rights organizations. For example, the Tunisian League for the Defense of Human Rights (Ligue tunisienne des droits de l'homme, LTDH), the first human rights group in the Arab world, played a more important role than oppositional parties in criticizing the ruling party, the Democratic Constitutional Rally (Rassemblement Constitutionnel Démocratique), in the 1990s and 2000s (Langohr 2004). In 2015, LTDH became one of the four organizations that constitute the

Table 5.1 The complex coexistence of civil society and undemocratic states

	Explanation	Cases	Features of the state	Features of the civil society
Opposition and contestation	Associations and individuals raise demands and directly challenge the state or create an oppositional social space	The Polish civil society in the 1970s; the Muslim Brotherhood; human rights advocacy organizations; dissidents	Strong state with limited space for associations; weak state with partial or nominal election system	Civil society is sustained and assisted by unofficial cultures, such as religions
Compromise and negotiation	Associations and individuals refrain from using language like "democracy" and choose unofficial political cultures that are tolerated by the state	Most associations in China and other authoritarian contexts	Strong state that needs associations' social service	Oppositional unofficial cultures are weak or unavailable
Conformity and adherence	Associations and individuals conform to and use the official ideology to frame their goals and demands	GONGOs[a] and many associations under authoritarianism	Strong state that adopts corporatism	Oppositional unofficial cultures are weak or unavailable
Silence and avoidance	Associations and individuals avoid addressing political issues and practice self-censorship	Most associations and individual participants in civil society engagement	Any undemocratic state	This culture can exist in any civil society in undemocratic contexts

Note: [a] GONGOS are "government-organized nongovernmental organizations," an oxymoron examined below.

"Tunisian National Dialog Quartet," which won the Nobel Peace Prize for its "decisive contribution to the building of a pluralistic democracy in Tunisia in the wake of the Jasmine Revolution of 2011" (Norwegian Nobel Institute 2015).

Many oppositional associations incorporate various other cultures, especially religious and spiritual beliefs and practices, into their public expressions and practices. In other words, they have "hybrid civil codes" (Lo and Fan 2010), sometimes even holding beliefs and norms of interactions that can be regarded by Western civil society actors as antidemocratic or illiberal.

China's Falun Gong, a spiritual movement, is such a case. The name of the movement literally means "exercises of the dharma wheel." Its core beliefs and practices combine various elements from Buddhism and Taoism. It built an extensive, hierarchical network of groups and associations in just a few years (Junker 2019). When the state media and scientists began to criticize Falun Gong as "feudal superstitions," the members launched their protests, which culminated in a large-scale sit-in around Zhongnanhai, the compound where China's central state and Chinese Communist Party are located. This led to the party-state's crackdown, and some Falun Gong practitioners among Chinese diasporas continued resistance outside China. Although the movement sometimes frames its values in the language of the culture of democracy, such as human rights, religious freedom, and so on, its internal norms are highly hierarchical and even follow the model of the personality cult. The movement also uses political vocabularies and propaganda techniques that ironically resemble those used by its enemy, the Chinese Communist Party.

Other cases of oppositional civil associations also show similar complexity in their cultural expressions and actions. For example, the Muslim Brotherhood in Egypt started as an Islamist organization that attempted to realize its ideological goals in political activities to build a new political system based on sharia (Islamic law) and against Western values (Wickham 2015). A critical juncture in the history of the Brotherhood was the 1980s, when the group expanded its involvement in Egyptian civil society and increasingly used the language of democracy and pluralism to challenge the regime. A particularly significant step for the Brotherhood was to join various professional associations, such as syndicates for doctors, engineers, and lawyers, and faculty clubs at universities. Within less than a decade, the Brotherhood gained majority seats on the boards of those associations, and a new generation of Brotherhood activists – the Islamic Trend leaders and activists – practiced and demonstrated their organizational and electoral skills and expanded their scope to address issues about non-Brotherhood members, such as junior professionals' jobs and incomes. Moreover, they used the syndicates to organize workshops and conferences on public issues and to communicate with the government, NGOs, and reporters. Consequently, the Islamic Trend people broke out of the Brotherhood's original networks and interacted across group boundaries, practicing what Tocqueville would call the "art of association."

Through participation in civil society, the Brotherhood accumulated networks and experience and later got involved in electoral politics. In the 2005 parliamentary elections, it became the first de facto oppositional party of Egypt in modern times, under Hosni Mubarak's regime. During the "Arab Spring" of 2011, the Brotherhood was not only involved in the protest but also formed the Freedom and Justice Party, which won the parliamentary election. In 2012, the Brotherhood's candidate, Mohamed Morsi, became the first democratically elected president in Egypt.

Correspondingly, the Brotherhood's "habits of the heart" also changed. The Islamic Trend leaders tended to recognize the importance of human rights and freedoms and used the language of democracy and pluralism. One of them said, for example:

> Those of us in the new generation, we studied and read widely and we interacted with those outside the circles of the Islamic movement. This had a huge effect on our thinking. We talked about human rights, respect for human life, democracy, and freedom. We saw that totalitarian regimes are based on a lack of respect for human life, and hence the solution is democracy and freedom. Through our readings, through our travels, and through our participation in public life, we asked questions, we investigated, and we realized that the problem of the system was that it was not democratic. And when we reviewed

the legacy of Muslim political thought, we found no contradiction between democracy and Islam. (Wickham 2015: 65)

Scholars used the "participation/moderation" thesis to explain these changes: participation in civil society and electoral politics makes the group's ideology less radical and more plural and democratic. This argument is much in line with neo-Tocquevillianism, especially the "school of democracy" thesis, but it shares with neo-Tocquevillianism the same problem of linearity and simplicity. As Wickham's detailed study points out, although participation in the civil society and later electoral politics did change the Brotherhood's political culture, the changes that happened to the Brotherhood were uneven, inconsistent, and not always in line with expectations from the liberal democracy perspective (Wickham 2015).

For example, like Catholicism in Poland, Islamism also provides an important framework for the Brotherhood activists to reinterpret a Western culture of democracy in their own terms. Nevertheless, unlike the Catholic interpretation that sustained the culture of democracy, the Islamist interpretations caused conflicts and dilemmas in the ideas and actions of the Brotherhood. Debates broke out over a few crucial questions, for example, how to embrace both Islamism and modernity, how to reconcile political strategies with the Brotherhood's rigid ideology, and how to distinguish itself from more militant Islamist organizations (Wickham 2015).

Another complexity is that the culture of democracy as a norm of interaction developed weakly within the Brotherhood. The internal culture and structure still follow religious piety and hierarchy instead of critical thinking and open debate, although the younger generations have tried to challenge that culture (Wickham 2015: 152–3). The old guard in the Brotherhood largely remained unchanged in their conservative views and practices and acted against the reformists in the organization. Thus, cursory outside observers, particularly Western politicians, often misunderstand the cultural paradoxes and tend to regard the complexity as an ideological pretense of being more open and liberal.

Compromise and Negotiation

Most associations under undemocratic states, however, do not directly challenge the states, especially when the states and associations are functionally interdependent: the states need the services the associations provide, and the associations need the states' institutional permission and resources. Both sides want to keep the interaction going. The states apparently have the upper hand, and thus associations often refrain from raising claims and expressing ideas that might be interpreted by the states as politically sensitive or even subversive. The associations carefully choose alternative cultural expressions to tell the state who they are and what they aim to achieve.

Much of Chinese civil society practice since the 1989 Tiananmen incident has been a typical case of compromise and negotiation. After the Tiananmen incident, as the state relaunched the economic reform, whirlwind changes in the economy and society generated unprecedented demands for social services and effective communications. The state, despite its unparalleled prowess, simply could not meet all the demands and thus delegated some of its social functions to non-state organizations. Correspondingly, the state's grip on the society was loosened. The authoritarian Chinese state's multifaceted aspect also led to some room for civil society. Within the state system, different actors with multiple levels of authority and various agendas interact with civil society in various ways, according to their judgment on the issue areas of the organizations, situations of interactions, and local contexts (Kang and Han 2008; Teets 2014; Hsu 2017). In response, associations, especially informal, unregistered organizations, used nonconfrontational strategies to survive in the crevices in the system (Spires 2011; Hildebrandt 2013; Hu et al. 2016; Xu 2017). Consequently, after a few years of inactivity following Tiananmen, the Chinese civil society restarted and rapidly grew. In 1988, there were only 4,446 officially registered associations in China; in 2018, there were more than 816,000, a 180-fold increase (Ministry of Civil Affairs of People's Republic of China 2019). This number did not include countless grassroots associations and small groups which actively participate in various public activities but do not bother to gain a legal status.

Nevertheless, the Chinese state did not let down its guard. The memory of Tiananmen and the fall of Communism remained fresh. To control the booming civil society, the state formalized some regulations in the 1990s, for example, the "dual-management" system, under which an NGO must be registered with both the Civil Affairs, the bureau in charge of organizations, and another government bureau or agency. In effect, this regulation strengthened the state's surveillance and management of the NGOs and made associations' legal registration even more difficult (Hsu et al. 2016). In the early 2000s, the "Color Revolutions" in Georgia, Ukraine, and Kyrgyzstan were interpreted by the Chinese state as a challenge of civil societies to authoritarianism. These events further perturbed the state.

In this complex coexistence situation, the authoritarian state demarcates a boundary between what are acceptable cultural expressions and what are not. Some part of the boundary is clear, whereas other parts remain fuzzy. Many associations resort to unofficial cultural expressions that are accepted by the state as legitimate, nonthreatening moral discourses of justification. They avoid alarming labels, such as "nongovernmental organization," which could be interpreted by the government as "anti-government organization." Instead, they identify themselves as "public welfare organizations" (*gongyi zuzhi*), which downplays the political implications of their actions. It is also more action-oriented, "workable" for the associations who want to make a difference in a less conducive context (Wu 2017). These cultural expressions and identities also depend on the situation. In private conversations or interviews with researchers, some volunteers unequivocally define their purposes and values as "democracy, equality, and participation." In seeking accesses to a university, however, the same volunteers present their association as an organization with a goal to train students and nurture their work ethics, without any mention of democratic values (Xu and Ngai 2011).

Sometimes, associations uncritically accept the state's moral discourses, which are used to justify its inability to provide adequate social services. One of these moral discourses promoted by the Chinese state is *aixin* ("loving heart"), which encourages ordinary citizens and civil associations to shoulder their moral responsibility to help others in need. The warm expression *aixin*, however, diverts public attention from the problems with the state's welfare policies, such as lack of basic education, as well as social problems like social inequality, which causes misery among the people they serve. NGO practitioners sometimes do not realize the political implications of this moral expression. For example, a fifth-grader from a migrant family, a recipient of an NGO's aids, wrote a letter to the NGO worker to express her gratitude. The NGO worker felt moved by the touching letter but did not realize that the girl interpreted the basic education as something like a "gift" rather than her basic right. A "gift" is something offered by the state and organizations if they are willing to do so, and the student was instructed to be grateful for the "gift." A "right," in contrast, is what the student is entitled to. Giving a gift without granting the right is to strengthen the giver's power. As a result, "once the relationship between volunteers, NGO workers, and rural migrants has been moralized, unequal social relations are performed, confirmed, reproduced, and legitimized" (Zhan 2020: 76).

Conformity and Adherence

In some contexts, the undemocratic states develop a "corporatist" strategy to control civil societies by favoring some associations over others, through developing "clientelism" and using GONGOs, an oxymoron that refers to "government-organized nongovernmental organizations," as mentioned in table 5.1. The favored associations, in return, adopt the official, undemocratic ideology of the state to justify their claims and frame their goals, and help the state set the agenda and expectations for other associations.

In cases of "clientelism," some state actors, either agencies or individual officials, offer security and resources to some associations but not others through vertical, informal relations. In return, the associations contribute their loyalty to the state and personal assistance to the officials (Scott 1972). For example,

Amaney A. Jamal's research shows that the vibrant associational life in the Palestine-controlled West Bank translates into clientelism instead of horizontal trust or universal values of equality (Jamal 2007). The West Bank boasts one of the richest associational landscapes in the Arab world. By 1999, 20 percent of its population were involved in associations and expressed their opinions and visions about many political issues, from ending the Israeli Occupation before the Oslo Accords to improving the post-Oslo Palestinian society. Nevertheless, the PNA (Palestinian National Authority) under Yasser Arafat's leadership governed the civil society through patronage, clientelism, and even personalism. The civil society quickly became polarized into those that supported the PNA and those that did not. If a sports club wanted to secure some financial and institutional support, it had to be part of Arafat's clientelist network. In fact, associations usually functioned as a gateway for their members to connect to the PNA to obtain resources that otherwise would have been unavailable.

The high-level trust in the pro-PNA associations, however, was not "horizontal" – among members and in other associations – but vertical and hierarchical: connecting to the state and powerful officials. Thus, members of those associations felt content with their particularistic connections and did not feel the need to engage in public activities to improve the society in general, let alone pursuing democracy (Jamal 2007: 80–1). The anti-PNA associations paid a heavy price: few government resources, limited room, and even a low level of interpersonal trust among their members, because they were unable to get them jobs and opportunities.

GONGOs are surrogates set up by states to represent a certain issue area and to limit and even expel non-state organizations (Brook and Frolic 1997; Unger 2008). GONGOs are mostly extensions of the undemocratic state and unsurprisingly show an even more explicit adherence to the official ideology. For example, the Red Cross Society of China, a typical GONGO, is directly controlled by the Civil Affairs bureau. Its offices are usually in the Civil Affairs buildings, and its employees are on the government's payroll. Through the Red Cross and its pervasive networks of branches, the state can dominate some fields, such as public fundraising and disaster response. The Red Cross also expectedly follows the official ideology to discuss its goals and meanings, for example, as its website claims, "to implement [President] Xi Jinping's thought on the Socialism with Chinese characteristics in the new age, to adhere to the Party's leadership, to follow the right direction," in addition to some universal claims about health, humanism, international cooperation, and so on (Xinhua News Agency 2019).

"Hybrid" regimes or "competitive authoritarian states" even more regularly use corporatism instead of heavy-handed crackdown or direct control because such methods may cause a backlash in a half-open society. Consequently, some sectors of civil society collaborate with the state and thus comply with the interaction norms of conformity and adherence, whereas other sectors of civil society remain oppositional and contestant. For example, Turkey's Women and Democracy Association (Kadin ve Demokrasi Derneği; KADEM), a pro-government organization, centers its policy on the conservative policies of the ruling Justice and Development Party (Adalet ve Kalkınma Partisi; AKP) (Yabanci 2019). KADEM's guiding values are focused on women's role in families and in society to help inculcate the youth with moral values. It provides legal advice and support to survivors of domestic violence but only by cherry-picking: mostly helping those women who were either veiled or underage but not those who were wearing skirts or shorts, or the transgendered. A representative of KADEM admits: "LGBT issues and religious values are our red lines" (Yabanci 2019: 298).

Complexity, however, reaches its highest level in those cases in which conformity to an authoritarian or hybrid state does not extinguish but rather helps advance the culture of democracy. In those cases, the states might strategically open access for disadvantaged groups to participate in public life and political decisions, although they may retain their authoritarian and repressive practices on other aspects. In the aftermath of the Rwanda genocide (chapter 6), the Rwandan Patriotic Front (RPF) emerged as the ruling party of the post-genocide state. Despite its effort to paint a self-image as a champion of post-conflict reconciliation and even democratization, the RPF-led state was at best a hybrid regime, with some democratic components, such as elections, and increasingly apparent authoritarian practices, such as cherry-picking candidates, intimidating some candidates, human rights abuses, and even violent revenge on the Hutu. Moreover, the RPF perceived civil society as a helper for and an extension of the state and formally turned this notion into law in 2001. Under the law, civil associations must comply with the state's strategic ends or face punishment (Burnet 2008: 375–6).

Nevertheless, the RPF's gender policy was more than just a pretense. The major leaders of RPF were refugees to Uganda, where the state made progressive policies and laws on gender and other issues. Influenced by their political experience in Uganda, the RPF leaders led efforts to draft and pass a new constitution that increased the quota of female representatives in the Senate and the Chamber of Deputies. In the Chamber of Deputies (the lower house of parliament), for example, twenty-four out of eighty members must be women who are elected by women voters only. The 2003 election saw these twenty-four within the quota plus fifteen women representatives through general election, which almost "held up half the sky" of the Chamber. Women's movements, especially the umbrella organization Collectifs Pro-Femmes/Twese Hamwe (Pro-Femmes), actively participated in the process of drafting the constitution.

This strong legislative presence of women also reflected the social changes before and after the genocide. In general, Rwanda suffered a massive loss of males in the civil war, and in the wake of the genocide 70 percent of the population were female. Women consequently took a much more active role in families and public life than before the genocide. Women's organizations had also been participating in rebuilding the nation after the genocide. Organizations like the Association of the Widows of April 1994 helped the widows to gain their advocacy power and obtain outside aid directly. Before the 2003 constitution, women's organizations like Pro-Femmes had already gained experience in using the authoritarian state for their advocacy and working with the state on legal issues such as the "Inheritance Law" in 1999, which expands the legal rights of women. The RPF state, despite its authoritarian nature, also used its progressive gender policies to reap political and diplomatic benefits, including international accolades for President Paul Kagame, foreign aid organizations' funds, and fending off criticisms for its human rights abuse on other issues (Burnet 2008). In sum, since an undemocratic state can be multifaceted and sometimes strategically grant civil society access and opportunities for their own political purposes, civil society may seize those opportunities to advance its own agenda by conforming to the state's policies and ideologies.

Silence and Avoidance

Keeping silent about the causes of people's suffering and avoiding controversial and dangerous topics happens in all civil societies, as I have discussed in chapter 3. But such silence is more deafening in the context where the undemocratic regime heavily restricts political expressions and actions.

Some cases of silence are responses to subtler methods of state control. In those cases, the undemocratic state takes only few measures but creates a political atmosphere in which everyone dreads speaking out because they know the imminent danger if they do. For example, the state uses high-profile cases of crackdown to create a chilling effect to deter other actors who have the same intention to challenge the state. In the long run, a "spiral of silence" forms in those contexts: the more repressive the context, the less you talk about political issues; the less you talk about political issues, the higher the cost of talking about or acting on them. Eventually, you do not even have the desire to talk about them (Xu 2017). This leads to a higher concentration of associations' work on politically "safe" issues and self-censorship among citizens. In some cases, avoiding certain issues is just the other side of adherence to the state ideology. KADEM in Turkey, as mentioned above, consciously avoids LGBT issues and distances itself from feminism by emphasizing women's familial role and moral values instead of rights (Yabanci 2019).

Even subtler cases, however, are those in which the undemocratic state does not have a clearly defined standard on which actions are allowed or forbidden (Stern and O'Brien 2012). In China's case, the party-state often sends out contradictory signals and changes its standards on censorship, and different state actors sometimes have different agendas. Consequently, an action allowed at one time, in one place, by one bureau may be forbidden and punished at other times, in other places, by other bureaus. This significant level of uncertainty leaves civil society actors, including journalists, human rights lawyers, and NGOs, in a state of confusion and anxiety. To speculate about what is allowed and what is forbidden in such situations, civil society actors use what Stern and Hassid term "control parables," stories about other actors who got into political trouble due to the unpredictable state control (Stern and Hassid 2012). As the state never clearly specifies its rules, the main purpose of control parables is to generate "a set of imagined rules designed to prevent future clashes with authority" (2012: 1241).

The result of control parables is ironically the proliferation of more forbidden zones than the officially claimed ones. For example, a chief editor of a newspaper was fired because, as the state claimed, the paper criticized the official English translation of a government document. But few journalists were convinced that the editor was punished so severely for such an insignificant reason. Many came up with their own explanations, mostly about the topics the paper had reported on. Such control parables made later journalists think twice about reporting on those topics. Consequently, control parables work as a mechanism of self-censorship, amplifying the silence and avoidance in a context where the state's control is arbitrary and unpredictable. The spiral of silence is also exacerbated when the civil society actors tend to exchange parables instead of speaking out publicly.

The Fall of Hong Kong: Precariousness of Complex Coexistence

The complex-coexistence paradigm in the scholarship on civil society emerged as an antidote to the simplistic view that civil societies are and should always be in conflict with undemocratic states.

It pays great attention to the nuances and variations of civil societies under authoritarianism. Nevertheless, it is equally important to keep in mind the fragility and precariousness of such coexistence, especially against the background that undemocratic regimes have become more robust and determined in the past decades. In addition to direct intervention and heavy-handed crackdown, the authoritarian state may also use indirect interventions, such as manufacturing public opinion, spreading disinformation, establishing surrogates to instigate conflicts, and so on. Consequently, such complex coexistence collapses and degrades into an "uncomplex" total control by the state.

No case illustrates this point better than Hong Kong. In 1997, the People's Republic of China regained its sovereignty over Hong Kong from the United Kingdom and turned it into a "Special Administrative Region" (HKSAR), a locality with a high degree of autonomy under a special political-legal framework known as "one country, two systems." The Basic Law of HKSAR, the legal equivalent of a constitution, protects the freedoms of speech, assembly, and protest, which are absent in the Mainland. Hong Kongers were also promised the prospect of the democratic election of its chief executive, but were offered no specific plan to put this into practice. This "one country, two systems" arrangement contained a fair amount of vagueness, but at that time the vagueness was regarded as a creative solution finessed by China and the UK. Since then, however, its drawbacks have become evident in a series of world-shaking events.

In 2014, China's National People's Congress (NPC) ruled that the right to nominate candidates for the chief executive should be limited to a 1,200-member committee, which, to a large extent, had been deliberately configured to ensure the results that China's central government wanted to see. This ignited Hong Kongers' long-time grievances and anger, intensified their demand for genuine universal suffrage, and triggered a massive protest and an occupation of a central place in the city's downtown. The protest and occupation were dubbed the "Umbrella Movement" because of the yellow umbrellas used by protesters to shield themselves from tear gas. The movement, however, was suppressed at the end of 2014.

An even greater and more intense movement resurrected in 2019 when the HKSAR government proposed a bill to amend two existing laws to allow the chief executive to transfer fugitives to Hong Kong back to Taiwan, Macau, and Mainland China, the latter two of which were currently excluded in the existing laws. An apparent legal implication was that a person could be extradited to Mainland China if this person was accused of a crime under the Mainland legal system; there was a possibility that a political dissident might be extradited. A more significant implication was that the bill might eventually ruin Hong Kongers' rule of law and legal autonomy. The proposal provoked a storm in Hong Kong. Hong Kongers flooded onto the streets and held a spontaneous protest on a scale unseen in the city's history. As the police intensified their crackdown by frequent use of tear gas, the protesters resorted to more militant ways of defiance. College and high-school students, geared up with gas masks, clubs, and Molotov cocktails, engaged in street fights with the police and barricade battles on university campuses. This round of rebellion was brutally suppressed; protesters were arrested and convicted.

In 2020, the NPC passed a Hong Kong National Security Law, which made it illegal for literally anyone in any place in the world to do anything that can be interpreted by the NPC or HKSAR government as jeopardizing the "national security" of China. Although it remains unclear how the National Security Law can be enforced in places outside Hong Kong, it effectively terminated any form of anti-government activism and placed unprecedented restrictions on Hong Kong's civil society. Activists were convicted, university student associations disbanded, newspaper owners arrested. Hong Kongers' pursuit of democracy came to a halt, and "one country, two systems" became little more than a political charade.

Before these upheavals, Hong Kong's civil society was regarded as one of the most vibrant in East Asia. Many civil society figures, like Kin-man Chan, mentioned at the beginning of this book, also have been instrumental in training associations and activists in Mainland China. The relatively independent public sphere in Hong Kong provided Mainland intellectuals with venues to publish commentaries and articles that were unable to appear in the Mainland Chinese media. Nevertheless, since China and the UK agreed on the return, Hong Kongers have never stopped their doubts about whether the Chinese state would keep its promise. All their doubts turned into reality in 2020.

Some cultural sociological studies before the events in the 2010s had already hinted at this tragic ending. Many of them follow the CST approach. Lo and Bettinger's study of political cartoons before China's 1997 takeover of Hong Kong had suggested that there was not a shared set of cultural codes in the public sphere in Hong Kong; such an absence of universalistic codes makes public engagement with each other in debates less effective (Lo and Bettinger 2009).

One can make a quick comparison to the American Civil Rights movement in Alexander's theoretical analysis (Alexander 2006): Civil Rights succeeded because the Black fight was supported by the universal values of equality and freedom intrinsically rooted in the civil sphere in the North. Mainland China, however, was not Hong Kong's "North"; rather, it was Hong Kong's "South," a place where the civil sphere remains underdeveloped, if not absent. Individual freedom, democracy, and autonomy are not in the Mainland's official political culture. Without a sovereign state, the communicative and regulative institutions in the Hong Kong civil sphere are too weak to resist the invasion of Mainland capital, political force, and bureaucratic and legislative control.

It is against this structural background that some more recent writings began to use the CST to explain the struggle and dramatic fall of Hong Kong's civil society in the period 2014–20. They were published after the 2014 Umbrella Movement and before the 2019 anti-extradition-bill movement, but they provided insights that remain valuable and relevant to the current situation. Agnes Ku analyzes two cases of contentions, the Public Order Ordinance protest in 2000 and the Umbrella Movement in 2014, and finds that binary codes about legality, justice, and civility were at the center of the protests (Ku 2019). For the pro-Beijing elites, civility meant lawfulness in the discourse of law and order. For the protesters, civility meant civil disobedience, which was rooted in the rule of law rather than public order. Clashes of the two discourses, however, were not just about words but had real-world consequences. The protesters formed a community based on the universal norms of civility and solidarity and enacted their understanding of law and civil society in activism like occupying public spaces in 2014, whereas the Beijing and HKSAR governments continued to ignore the institutional code about the rule of law and focused on the uncivil manner of individual actions such as vandalism.

This irreconcilable tension between two sets of codes gave rise to militant radicalism based on a local identity as Hong Kongers instead of a national identity as Chinese. At a deeper level, as Junker and Chan show, the democratic codes have a twist: universal claims of liberty are tied to the particularistic, subnational identity of being Hong Kongers, whereas the uncivil side of the codes is attached to the Mainland government and could be extended to Mainlanders (Junker and Chan 2019). Sometimes, this twist has a "dark turn": anti-Mainland-Chinese sentiments drew on a discriminatory image of Mainlanders as uncivil – in both manners and political culture – while Hong Kongers are believed to be law-abiding and civilized. This observation further testifies to the CST that the civil sphere has its exclusionary ideas and practices lurking under its universalistic claims. On the other hand, such exclusions were also Hong Kongers' response to the central state's deliberate manipulation and instigation of the Mainland public discourses, which turned significantly hostile in the 2014–20 period.

The elephant in the room is the Chinese state. Its decisive role in shaping civil societies constitutes a challenge to the complex coexistence paradigm. This paradigm makes sense when the authoritarian state strategically allows some room for civil society for its own purposes or simply lacks the ability to maintain its control. But, by definition, authoritarianism is not a type of regime with intrinsic flexibility and responsiveness. Moreover, as Linz and Stepan almost prophetically asserted in 1996 (Linz and Stepan 1996: 18–19), a year before China's regaining sovereignty over Hong Kong, Hong Kong's democratic aspiration is not sustained by a separate sovereign state, and the "one country, two systems" model does not guarantee Hong Kong a constitutionally autonomous state. "Without a sovereign state, there can be no secure democracy," Linz and Stepan argue (1996: 19). Thus, the fall of Hong Kong civil society is a wake-up call for theorists and observers: the authoritarian state's flexible and subtle control can be overridden by more draconian methods when the state is robust, unchecked, and determined. Flexibility was its old tactic; repression is the new normal.

6

Global Civil Society

A holy gathering! peaceful all:
No threat of war, no savage call
For vengeance on an erring brother!
But in their stead the godlike plan
To teach the brotherhood of man
To love and reverence one another,
As sharers of a common blood,
The children of a common God! (Whittier, 1839)

The "holy gathering" described in this poem was the "General Anti-Slavery Convention," better known as the "World Anti-Slavery Convention," in London in 1840 (Maynard 1960). It was organized by one of the first INGOs, the "British and Foreign Anti-Slavery Society" (later renamed "Anti-Slavery International"). In terms of the number and the importance of delegates, this conference surpassed many international assemblies at the time. About 500 delegates attended the meeting, mostly from the UK and the US. The organizers were well-known British abolitionists, including the English Quaker Joseph Sturge, and among the American delegates were William Lloyd Garrison and Wendell Phillips, two prominent figures in America's abolitionist movement. The convention took place long before the International Committee of the Red Cross (ICRC) held its first international convention in 1863.

Before "global civil society" became a buzzword in the late twentieth century, global civil society had already taken shape in its essential forms: INGOs, activists traveling across national borders, and international conferences. More importantly, the poem quoted above, by American abolitionist John Greenleaf Whittier, articulated universal values at the global scale: delegates from different countries were "children of a common God"; they gathered, with "love and reverence" to one another, for a "godlike plan," that is, to free slaves around the world. These were not empty words. In its long history, Anti-Slavery International participated in various actions against slavery, forced labor, human trafficking, and other issues beyond the traditional meaning of slavery.

Nevertheless, the World Anti-Slavery Convention also signified some cultural paradoxes that remain central in today's global civil society. All the organizers and delegates were white men from only a few major Western countries (the UK, US, and France) and UK colonies. If this problematic regional representativeness could be justified by the fact that abolitionism at the time mostly occurred in those countries, then the convention's hostility toward women contradicted its universal claim. American women had been active in the abolitionist movement and were nominated by their local organizations to attend the convention. But some American delegates had been opposing William Garrison's agenda of associating other "radical" issues such as women's rights with abolitionism. They wrote to the British organizers to bar American women abolitionists from attending the meeting. Joseph Sturge and other British organizers agreed and announced that only male delegates were expected. On the very first day of the convention, American delegate Wendell Phillips moved that women delegates should be admitted, but his motion was opposed by the majority of the delegates, especially the British. Consequently, American women delegates were banned from participating in the discussion and only allowed to observe the meeting from the visitors' gallery. In protesting against the decision, William Lloyd Garrison, who arrived late, chose to sit with the women delegates without participating in most of the discussions. A positive, unintended outcome of this convention, however, was that the women delegates who met at the convention, including Lucretia Mott and Elizabeth

Cady Stanton, were stimulated by the gender discrimination and organized the first women's rights convention eight years later in Seneca Falls, New York.

This "women question" in one of the earliest INGO meetings suggested the contradiction between the "global culture of democracy" and the fault lines of identities. The culture of democracy seems to culminate in its global form because its core values get their best illustration in globally universal statements: liberty means liberty to all people around the world; equality should be achieved at the global scale; and tolerance means to include everyone on the planet regardless of their nationalities. The early INGOs like Anti-Slavery International pursued these values in their undoubtedly heroic actions, such as the effort to free slaves, but the values of inclusiveness and equality were not extended to their fellow activists of the opposite sex. Here we see not only the limitations of universal values but also the discrepancies between two kinds of cultures: values in the cultural structure (the universalism in abolitionism) and culture as norms of interactions (the ways the abolitionists treated their fellow activists).

Global civil society is deeply rooted in the processes of world history long before our times. But its development accelerated in the 1990s, when the interconnectedness of the world exponentially grew thanks to the end of the Cold War, new technology in transportation and communications, and various social-political changes around the world (Kaldor 2003). This acceleration dramatizes and makes visible some of the problems intrinsic in global civil society, which, as the case of Anti-Slavery International shows, were already evident in its early stages. Cultural sociology examines the paradoxes, contradictions, and developments in the culture of democracy at the global level. "Global" here is not a clichéd adjective. Nor does it mean merely non-Western; this book has discussed many non-Western cases. Rather, it refers to the actors, processes, institutions, and discourses beyond national borders and between different nation-states, such as INGOs, volunteers who work outside their home countries, international networks of organizations, and cultural values, ideas, and practices about people as residents of the world as opposed to citizens of nations.

In examining global civil society, cultural sociologists do not use a simplistic, homogeneous concept of "local culture" as opposed to "global norms." Such a concept often assumes a consensual, static nature for a non-Western society and downplays the variations and conflicts in such a culture. Thus, this essentialist concept often justifies a naïve "respect" for the exotic "local culture" in the Western imagination and an uncritical acceptance of blatantly wrong practices such as rape. In contrast, cultural sociologists use the theoretical tools that have been discussed in previous chapters, offering differential, dynamic images of global civil society, including its progress and paradoxes, achievements as well as dilemmas.

World Culture and Global Civil Society

The *world culture* theory (also termed *world society* or *world polity* theory) is a major theoretical contribution to the cultural sociological agenda on global civil society. John W. Meyer laid its conceptual foundation. Meyer views *world culture* or the "cultural dimension of world society" as an "*institution*", "the cognitive and ontological models of reality that specify the nature, purposes, technology, sovereignty, control, and resources of nation-states and other actors" (Meyer et al. 1997: 149). World culture is institutionalized into rules, ethics, and norms defined formally by international organizations' regulations and international laws. These institutions are "scripts" for social actors, including individuals, organizations, and nation-states, but the actors' actions also constantly write and rewrite the scripts.

Meyer's theory emphasizes the global feature of culture, as represented in the universalistic values of rational actors, progress, fairness, equality, and so on. These world cultures regulate a "stateless world," where there is no single world government but many nation-states, organizations, and individuals and their networks. World culture as an institution defines the rules for them to maintain a relatively stable order instead of plunging into a war of all against all. In this sense, the concept "world culture" is a concept of "culture in structure," in which the "culture" is a global system of symbols, meanings, and rules.

Because the world culture regulates the world at the global level, Meyer points out, it must be universal instead of particularistic. The universalistic feature of world culture results in the remarkable similarities of states and organizations in different parts of the world. Most states have a legislature, administrative branch, armed forces, the justice system, and so on. Even government bureaus and agencies are similar, such as commerce, labor, transportation, treasury, and so forth. Organizations are even more similar, not only in their bureaucratic structures but also in their conformity to rules, ethics, and norms, which are often defined by some international organizations with no material power to enforce such rules. Such similarities ("isomorphism") indicate the existence of a universal culture, despite its local variations.

The world culture theory is in sharp contrast to other theories of globalization, especially the *world-system theory*, in which culture is secondary to material power and only functions as an instrument of legitimation or ideological battleground of the modern world-system. In this battleground, as the theory argues, world capitalism, the states in the core, and international governance organizations such as the International Monetary Fund (IMF) and World Bank use a series of ideologies, especially individualism and neoliberalism, to maintain their dominance over the periphery and semi-periphery countries and organizations (Wallerstein 2004). The world culture theory, however, asserts that culture is a primary and constitutive factor. World culture is a cultural frame at the global level, shaping various actors' worldviews, which tend to see the global world as a unitary system with universalistic norms and rules.

Civil society, especially INGOs, is central to the world culture theory. INGOs are the carriers of the world culture, promoting universal ideas and norms such as human rights, environmentalism, and universal education, and even regulating professional practices and activities. In a longitudinal study of 5,983 international organizations founded between 1875 and 1988, John Boli and colleagues found that measures of world development, such as exports, education enrollment, technological developments, and citizen rights, occur at the same time and strongly correlate with each other (covariance mostly above .90), across different levels of development. More importantly, those development measures are highly correlated with the number of INGOs founded at the same time, also with covariance coefficients above .90 (Boli and Thomas 1997). These unusually strong correlations cannot be explained by the world-system theory, which would predict a significant variation in the development across core and peripherical countries and simply have no explanation for the correlations with INGOs.

Boli and colleagues supplement this longitudinal statistical analysis with a historical analysis of the dialectic processes between the expansions of nation-states and world society. INGOs proliferated in the late nineteenth and early twentieth centuries, when both nation-states and European imperialism were also at their peak. The two world wars, in their destructive ways, enhanced the global consciousness and stimulated the further development of INGOs. INGOs gained their prestige and significant influence in the postwar years. Their functions concentrate in sectors like science, trade, technology, the environment, and sports. They have significantly shaped global technical standards, rules of war, population policy, women's rights, and so on.

In another study based on the same data, Boli and his colleagues examine who actually participates in the INGOs and whether such participation increases or decreases over time, a "bowling alone" question at the global level (Boli et al. 1999). Their findings confirm some conventional wisdom about global inequality. For example, participation and institutionalization are found with greater concentration in more developed countries. Nevertheless, there are also some counterintuitive findings: for example, the growth in INGO membership is universal, occurring among all categories of countries across numerous dimensions, and increases even more in non-Western regions. The world culture theory provides a powerful explanation: the concept of world citizenship, not necessarily in those exact words, spreads as a world culture and provides people around the world, including in less developed countries, with the necessary knowledge, resources, and habits of voluntaristic actions to participate in the global civil society.

The world culture theory also provides a new perspective on the relationships among INGOs, domestic NGOs, and nation-states. A conventional image is that grassroots NGOs spring up from local communities in non-Western societies to solve the pressing issues in their societies, such as environmental problems. Nevertheless, a study by David J. Frank, Wesley Longhofer, and Evan Schofer shows that this image is more a myth than reality (Frank et al. 2007). They examine a received storyline about environmentalism in Asia: that the serious environmental degradation across Asia provoked grassroots NGOs to enhance public awareness of the problems and to press their national governments for policy reforms. These researchers find that this story is only partially true. In fact, national chapters of INGOs of environmentalism took root in Asia before the rise of domestic NGOs in the 1980s–1990s. The national environmental agencies were founded by Asian governments after the UN's two environment conferences – in Stockholm in 1972 and in Rio in 1992 – rather than before. Thus, the authors argue that world society "provides both a global nursery and a world sprinkler system – nurturing domestic NGOs and policy reforms and then distributing them throughout the nation-states of Asia" (2007: 283).

The puzzle, then, is: why is there still a myth of spontaneous grassroots NGOs? Frank, Longhofer, and Schofer argue that it is because the idea of "autonomy" is built into the world culture. Such an idea emphasizes spontaneous, independent, and participatory functions of self-governing organizations in building national civil societies and the global community. It is part of the global culture of democracy. This "script" enables domestic NGOs to claim their authority based on their representation of the people in their countries instead of being the agents of international NGOs. In this sense, the myth of grassroots NGOs is not wrong but belies its institutional origins in the world culture.

Nation-states are also active participants in, instead of just receptors of, the world culture of environmentalism, as another study by Frank and his colleagues shows (Frank et al. 2000).

Cynics may raise a valid doubt: the states may just half-heartedly "perform" to enhance their reputation by paying lip service to universal values without improving their human rights record. For example, since World War II, more and more states have ratified international laws and treatises of human rights, but meanwhile, states' violations of those human rights have also been increasing (Hafner-Burton and Tsutsui 2005). Are those international treaties on human rights just nice but useless documents, since they do not seem to improve the situation?

To respond to these challenges, Emilie M. Hafner-Burton and Kiyoteru Tsutsui draw from the world culture approach to make two arguments (Hafner-Burton and Tsutsui 2005). First, the human rights norms are indeed weak: there are often no formal ways to enforce the international laws on nation-states except in sensational cases. Thus, it is true that states' ratification of human rights treaties works more like global window-dressing.

Second, nevertheless, the values and corresponding institutions about human rights do have impacts on nation-states, but through indirect ways. The human rights institution often gives activists and civil society organizations powerful cultural frames to pressure states to improve human rights practices. In this sense, international laws about human rights as world culture work through INGOs instead of directly on the states. The empirical evidence for this hypothesis is that states with more linkage to the global civil society (for example, with more INGO memberships) are more likely to respect human rights and take action to improve the situation in their countries.

Other studies complement the world culture theory by highlighting a reversing trend: the role of non-Western, grassroots groups' possible contributions to world culture, so that the diffusion of global values like human rights is no longer a unilateral process flowing from the West to the non-West. Rather, as Tsutsui's study of Japan's minorities movement shows, it is more a feedback loop, through which local activism and NGOs in the non-Western countries consolidate and expand world culture, in his case, the issue of human rights (Tsutsui 2017). Ethnic activism for the rights of Ainu, indigenous people in northern Japan, especially in Hokkaido, benefits from their participation in the global human rights forums and their encounters with indigenous groups in other parts of the world. Meanwhile, the disproportionate success of this small indigenous community (population around 24,000) offers hope and motivation for other such groups. Its success, together with that of other minority groups, compels the Japanese government to contribute to the UN Voluntary Fund for Indigenous Peoples.

Another group, Burakumin (meaning "people residing in hamlets"), a group of people who face discrimination based on their ancestors' occupation and outcaste status in pre-Meiji Japan, succeeds in expanding the existing global norms. UN human rights documents such as the Universal Declaration of Human Rights do not include explicit statements about caste-based discrimination against groups like Burakumin and India's Dalits. The Convention on the Elimination of All Forms of Racial Discrimination (CERD) did include a statement on "descent," but the Japanese government interpreted the term as "descent of national and ethnic origins" instead of social status. To counter the government's interpretation, Burakumin activists mobilized support from various international NGOs and the UN organizations and successfully made the CERD add a statement to confirm the meaning of "descent" based on social status, which, as the statement explicitly assures, includes groups like Burakumin.

An alternative theoretical explanation goes beyond the assumption that modernity started in the West, diffused to the rest of the world, and then back to the West. Rather, this argument asserts that different parts of the world may simultaneously experience the same historical process, which, however, takes place in an uneven way (Tuğal 2017). For example, some Islamic charity organizations in Turkey and Egypt draw on Islam but combine it with a neoliberal style: they highlight self-reliance and cultivation of individual responsibility, mobilize middle-class volunteerism, run on a business model to quantify their effects, and so on. Thus, the civil societies in the Islamic world are not an exception but part of the general trends that use religious ethics to respond to rationalization, capitalism, and centralization of power in states.

The diffusion of world culture, however, often encounters resistance from nationalism, authoritarianism, populism, religious extremism, and so on. Some non-Western governments and groups regard the diffusion as the expansion of a Western-imposed political agenda under the disguise of humanitarian aids and INGOs (Carothers and Brechenmacher 2014). A milestone event was the fall of Slobodan Milošević of Serbia. Western aid organizations put together a well-designed program with a large amount of money ($50 million to $100 million) to support Serbian activists, independent media, and oppositional parties. Foreign aid may not be the determining factor for the transition of Serbia, but its high-profile involvement alerted other authoritarian governments. The "Color Revolutions" in Georgia, Ukraine, and Kyrgyzstan further substantiated the caution by demonstrating the importance of private foundations in helping oppositional activism.

Thus, since the late 1990s and early 2000s, many governments have restricted foreign funding to domestic NGOs (Bromley et al. 2020). Sixty countries have passed laws to put restrictions on domestic organizations receiving foreign NGO funding. Such restrictions are more likely to occur in countries with a strong presence of illiberal or anti-Western organizations and governments. Among them, Hungary and Egypt are probably the most famous examples.

In 2014, Viktor Orbán, Hungary's prime minister, described NGO staff as "paid political activists who are trying to help foreign interests" and ordered raids of NGOs which received foreign grants (The Economist 2014). This move was just one of Orbán's "Stop Soros" plans; others include attempting to close the Central European University funded by George Soros and pushing the Congress to pass a law to ban any NGOs and individuals from helping illegal migrants seek asylum in Hungary. In Egypt, domestic NGOs played a crucial role in the "Arab Spring" movement that toppled Hosni Mubarak, only to find themselves a target of the Justice Ministry's investigation of their activities and funding sources, especially funds from foreign sources. Foreign funds were viewed by the authorities as money with hidden political agendas, "promoting American and Israeli interests." NGOs were raided and staff arrested (Christensen and Weinstein 2013). In other countries, politicians and ordinary people connected Western INGOs' cultural claims – universalism based on human rights and democracy – to the wars Western states actively launched beyond their borders. INGOs were seen not as guardian angels of a universal dream but as Trojan horses sent by the Western crusaders.

Culture in Global Actions and Local Practices

Another type of challenge the global culture of democracy encounters is in local, grassroots societies, during its interactions with individuals and organizations. Civil society actors, INGOs and individuals, need to overcome some institutional and cultural obstacles to achieve their goals. Donors' money needs to go through a chain of INGOs and local NGOs to take effect. INGOs and individual volunteers need to find "brokers," who know the local situation, can communicate with outsiders in Western languages, and work on their behalf. The donors, organizations, volunteers, and brokers are involved in this deeply meaningful, even idealistic civic engagement at both global and local levels. While they are pursuing the same broadly defined goals, for example, to prevent HIV/AIDS in a certain country, they have different visions, agendas, imaginations, levels of knowledge, motivations, priorities, and so on. At this level, the global culture of democracy is not only values and notions stated in the formal documents of INGOs, that is, "culture in structure," but also "culture in action," values and notions enacted and changed in people's actions.

Ann Swidler and Susan Cotts Watkins provide a detailed account of how "culture in action" works in the global effort to tackle the AIDS/HIV problems in Malawi, one of the least developed countries in the world (Swidler and Watkins 2017). Deeply motivated by their own moral imaginations, Western donors and INGOs arrive in Malawi but soon find themselves in a "cultural minefield." On some issues, such as helping AIDS orphans and fighting the stigma attached to AIDS patients, the Western donors and the brokers can work in tandem. Other issues, however, are "mines" that donors tiptoe to avoid but sometimes accidentally step upon.

Two such "mines" stand out. First, the issue of "vulnerable women." Western donors cherish a belief that women are vulnerable to men's lust, sex work, and thus the infection of AIDS. Thus, it is necessary to empower women to control their lives and bodies and thus achieve gender equality. This idea is the Holy Grail of development policies in general and is adapted from Western women's rights movements, even though, as Swidler and Watkins point out, data suggest that urban and wealthier women in Africa, who enjoy more gender equality, are more likely to be infected (2017: 141). The "vulnerable woman" image and the corresponding views about gender equality motivate donors and INGOs. Brokers and villagers agree to this in a general sense. But they also believe that the local moral order has been threatened by the so-called "mercenary women," such as "bar girls" or any women who are believed to have sex with married men in exchange for money and other resources. They are viewed as "rapacious women who divert men's money from their moral obligation to support their family, and in so doing, bring a fatal disease into the home, a disease that, it is assumed, will be swiftly transmitted to the men's innocent wives, and ultimately, leave their children orphans" (2017: 142).

A Westerner might immediately find this view problematic: why are men so innocently "helpless?" Why is the blame always put on women? Yet these reasonable questions do not resonate with villagers in Malawi. If a woman is found to have had sex with a married man and caught on site, villagers may rush to witness the angry wife beating the woman and to support the wife, and the man often gets away without any moral scruple. In everyday conversations, local elderlies express their worries about pornography, social and religious gatherings at night, and "sexy dressing." An old woman describes her worries in a way that links "sexy dressing" to "democracy" (2017: 149, italics added):

You know what, *democracy has destroyed everything, see the way they have dressed*, see the mini-skirts this makes men to get attracted with the legs, ending up proposing them and sleeping with them others put on tight clothing, trousers which all these things during our time was not happening since 1960's, 70's 80's, but since 1990's Oh!

Many elites also share this view. Patricia Kaliati, who once was Malawi's Minister of Gender, Child Development and Welfare, a pioneer for the empowerment of girls and prevention of domestic violence, reportedly – and she did not deny this – kidnapped and beat a woman who was said to have had sex with her husband. After that incident, Kaliati continued to hold high-ranking positions in the Malawian government (2017: 145–6).

Brokers, who are in between the Western INGOs and donors and the local norms, manage to reconcile the two worlds by speaking in different voices in different contexts. They do not oppose the empowerment view in their training sessions and other formal settings. This conformity could be sincere because the empowerment programs may bring benefits – such as schooling for girls – to the local society. But in informal settings, such as casual chats during breaks, they express the same view that some women are just too "empowered" and should be restrained.

The other cultural mine is the stories about exotic, "harmful" sex practices, for example, a widow must sleep with a paid "sexual cleanser" to drive away the spirit of her dead husband. The stories are often told by brokers and local elites to Westerners with an implication that such harmful practices should be blamed for the AIDS/HIV epidemic, even though no statistical evidence supports this accusation. More interestingly, the researchers found that villagers themselves, who are supposed to be active in those practices, rarely talk about them.

Why? Swidler and Watkins argue that the brokers and elites tell these stories for at least two reasons. First, their storytelling about exotic behaviors helps establish their cultural authority. Without the brokers' and elite's knowledge, as the stories imply, Westerners are unable to navigate the local situations. Second, they genuinely believe that these backward practices impede Malawi's progress and thus should be blamed for the AIDS epidemic. Therefore, the brokers and elites can use their knowledge to contribute to the battle against AIDS. Westerners try to avoid the impression of disrespect for local culture and, therefore, they quickly identify this cultural mine and tiptoe to circumvent it.

One might expect grassroots INGOs, those smaller organizations relying on limited budgets and individual volunteers, to have more advantages than large INGOs in presenting the aid recipients in more personal, less stereotypical ways and, thus, preventing paternalism and counterproductive interventions. This expectation is not unreasonable. Allison Schnable's study shows that grassroots INGOs offer "amateurs" – occasional volunteers instead of NGO staff members – three crucial things: the chance to work directly with beneficiaries, the opportunity to share their knowledge and skills, and a way to use their own lives as a model for success when they encourage beneficiaries to achieve mobility (Schnable 2021: 78–93). They are also able to convey messages about the global South through narratives about how they, as individual volunteers, interact with the recipients. This is why grassroots volunteering across borders attracts people who want to bypass the organizational labyrinths, see for themselves, and act on their beliefs.

Nevertheless, despite its authenticity, civic engagement through grassroots INGOs is greatly shaped by the social relationships and knowledge of the individual volunteers, which are in turn shaped by the macro-level social-cultural relationships between the global North and the South. Schnable records two such cases (Schnable 2021: 148–56). The first case is Leann, an elementary school teacher in Minnesota, who taught English in Tanzania as a volunteer for Activate Tanzania, a grassroots INGO. After she returned to the US, she taught her students about Tanzanian culture and society according to her understanding of the country. For example, she believes that the country's children are "poor in materials but rich in *ujamaa* (community)." The other case is a nine-year-old girl, Lindsey, a volunteer for Wellsprings of Hope. Lindsey miraculously raised $25,000 in only five months to build a classroom in Uganda. The story was interpreted by the organization and Lindsey's parents, relatives, and friends as "God working through the girl." As promised, Lindsey's parents bought her a trip to Uganda to see the newly built school.

These two stories are used by the volunteers themselves and the grassroots INGOs to inspire more engagement. Their emotional power and inspiration come from their authenticity: against all odds and from afar, individuals take small actions and raise small amounts of money that have tangible impacts on poor countries. But Leann spent only a few weeks in Tanzania, and Lindsey began to raise funds in accordance with imagined rather than real interactions with poor children in Uganda. Their limited contacts with the global South led to a giver-centered perspective in interpreting the meanings of volunteering: Leann emphasized her understanding of "Tanzanian culture" and her passion for teaching, and Lindsey's story stressed the miracle as God's working through her. The funds raised by Americans and the help from Americans are perceived as an easy solution to the countries' problems. In this sense, Schnable argues, the promises that grassroots INGOs offer – authenticity and compassion through personal relations – still conform to, instead of challenging, the Northern stereotypes of the South.

To be fair to INGOs: many of them take cultural sensitivity seriously and make an earnest effort to have "best practice plans." They test their advertisement campaign plans through a series of social scientific methods, such as focus group interviews, expert consultations, and so on. They also invite local people to see if their mock-ups are culturally appropriate. Their efforts convince donors and themselves that they have done what they can to avoid "cultural mines."

Nevertheless, plans still go awry. In his book on AIDS/HIV media campaigns in Ghana, Terence E. McDonnell records some comedic cases of unintended consequences of such best practice plans (McDonnell 2016). AIDS organizations distributed free female condoms as a preventive measure but soon found out that the condoms were made into jelly bracelets. "Use a condom" billboards were set up in heavily trafficked areas to maximize their visibility, but they were too high to be seen from inside of *trotros* (minibuses), which are the common transit option for many middle- and working-class people, the target audience of the campaign. A smartly designed billboard attempted to convince people that "Avoiding AIDS is as easy as ABC (Abstain, Be Faithful, and Condomise)," but some words painted in red had faded to near illegibility. Consequently, the billboard read, "Avoiding . . . as easy as ABC." Even the successful ones do not always succeed for the right reasons. For example, a brand of condom supported by AIDS organizations was popular because it minimized AIDS-related messages but claimed that the products could "unleash the burning passion within you."

All these are what McDonnell terms *cultural entropy*, the chaotic process in which well-designed plans fail to achieve their intended effects or are used for unintended purposes. The instrumental logic of organizations does not usually take cultural entropy into consideration when designing campaign plans. The "best practices" are often high on planning, low on monitoring actual effects. The complex cultural topography of the developing countries often makes the entropy even more unpredictable: scarce resources, poverty, various alternative cultural interpretations of health and science, and even infrastructure and facilities can derail the plans made by Western and domestic organizations. For example, if when walking on the street one has to look down to avoid open sewage, a high billboard just does not work. Or an AIDS-education ad on a bus shelter can be easily blocked by the clothes a street vendor hangs on the shelter.

At a deeper level, this failure to include cultural entropy in the INGOs' plans reflects an overconfidence in the rationality of human design and planning and inadequate attention to the materiality of a cultural object. Cultural objects are *objects*, McDonnell claims. This is not a statement of a truism. Rather, it points out a blind spot in academic discourses and NGOs' management culture: they often pay a lot of attention to the symbols and meanings a cultural object carries but ignore that such meanings are embodied in material objects, which could resist human beings' controlling effort.

Dilemmas of Humanitarianism

Humanitarianism is one of the best cases to illustrate the global culture of democracy. It starts with transcendental moral ideals, realizes the ideals in actions and organizations, and diffuses around the globe. These ideals are also clearly stated in some widely held principles: "impartiality, for they must give aid based on need, not on who is being helped or where they live; neutrality, for they must avoid appearing to act in ways that favor one side or another; and independence, for they must be unconnected to any party with a stake in the conflict" (Barnett 2011: 2). In short, humanitarianism is intended to be "above the fray."

Take the ICRC as an example (Finnemore 1999). This well-known international organization originated from individuals' actions out of their moral conscience. Henry Dunant, a wealthy Swiss businessman, witnessed the Battle of Solferino between French-Sardinian and Austrian armies on his business trip to Italy in 1859. Dunant was shocked by the tens of thousands of wounded and dying soldiers left without care on the battlefield. Instead of fleeing from the horrendous scene, Dunant acted like a Samaritan, organizing local people to set up makeshift hospitals and caring for the wounded soldiers. Later he wrote a book, *Un Souvenir de Solferino* (*A Memory of Solferino*), to describe his experience. The book also promoted the idea that qualified volunteering medical practitioners should set up a neutral and impartial relief organization to care for all wounded personnel in wars, regardless of which sides they were on. Moreover, Dunant proposed, a treaty should be signed by the states to recognize such a relief organization.

The book, published at his own expense and distributed to dignitaries, was a runaway success: it received enthusiastic responses from ruling families of European states, public figures like Victor Hugo, and news media. Dunant's idea of a neutral aid organization was supported by Gustave Moynier, then chairman of the Geneva Society for Public Welfare, who used the Society to realize this idea. Soon a committee of five men, including Dunant and Moynier, set up the International Committee to Aid the Military

Wounded, the precursor of ICRC. This five-man committee persuaded twelve states to sign the first Geneva Convention "for the Amelioration of the Condition of the Wounded in Armies in the Field" in 1864. Twelve states might not sound impressive, but it was a monumental achievement: an international treaty completely initiated by private individuals and their organizations, who managed to have representatives of the states sit down, discuss, and eventually agree to their idealist principles. Moreover, the 1864 treaty evolved into the Geneva Conventions (including four treaties and three protocols) about humanitarian practices in wars, such as protection of and care for the wounded, prisoners of war, and civilians.

World culture scholar Martha Finnemore argues that the remarkable success of the ICRC and the first treaty of the Geneva Conventions cannot be solely explained by the warring states' self-interested purposes, that is, because they wanted their soldiers to return to the battlefield and expected their enemies to let relief organizations treat the wounded prisoners of war (POWs) as a reciprocal action (Finnemore 1999: 152–3). The historical facts contradict this explanation. Medical science in the 1860s was not advanced enough to guarantee a full recovery of wounded soldiers to become useful again quickly. The states signed the treaty unilaterally, without a condition that other states would take reciprocal actions. In practice, national Red Cross organizations also took unilateral actions. For example, during the Russo-Japanese War, the Japanese National Red Cross treated Russian soldiers to prove their moral superiority without expecting the Russians to do the same (Dromi 2020: 73–4). Therefore, Finnemore argues, the world culture perspective offers a strong alternative explanation: the universal moral idea about human lives became an institution that quickly gained support from warring states and set the ground rules of wars.

The founders of the ICRC cherished some idealistic, if not radical, moral principles, about which even some followers and key figures of the Red Cross movement harbored doubts. Even more surprising was that such an idealistic, "above the fray" vision of universal human dignity appeared a mismatch for the times. In the second half of the nineteenth century, when the Red Cross movement started, a major war occurred in every decade in Europe. In the first half of the twentieth century, when the Red Cross movement gained its momentum, the world was suffering from tragedies and atrocities caused by two world wars. The prevalent intellectual atmosphere was more of a reflection on the dark side of human nature, as in Sigmund Freud, or the "death of God" leading to the loss of universal values and perspectives. This period also saw the rise of nationalism in Europe and around the world, which seemed to counter the moral universalism in the Red Cross model (Hobsbawm and Ranger 1983). How could such universal ideals be realized in organizations in such violent and distressing times? How could they spread globally amid carnage?

Shai M. Dromi provides an explanation based on a combination of cultural sociology and a Weberian historical sociology (Dromi 2020). He starts with the assertion that the emergence of a new social field, such as humanitarianism, "requires a preexisting belief system (religious or otherwise) that orients actors to believe that specific endeavors are so unique and essential that they require an independent social space" (Dromi 2020: x). More specifically, many of the founders of the ICRC, including Henry Dunant, were Calvinists who belonged to the Réveil, a "revival" movement of Christianity in Switzerland and France.

These common features were not accidental. Several doctrines of the Réveil had a direct influence on the Red Cross movement. The founders, as Réveil Calvinists, "view Christianity as a guiding ethic that civilizes nations, and they ascribe the cosmopolitan stance crucial for transnational humanitarianism to its tenets" (Dromi 2020: 37). The Réveil Calvinists highlighted the problems that modernity brought about, including poverty, moral corruption, and senseless wars. Like other Calvinists, such as Weber's Calvinist businessmen, the Réveil believed in action instead of mere beliefs: they actively engaged in worldly activities that changed and reformed the sorry state of the present society. This was the theological origin of the Red Cross's active intervention and volunteer initiatives. The Réveil espoused a suspicion toward the state and saw charity as a non-state, fundamental solution to many social problems. This suspicion of the state contributed much to the impartiality principle. Strong commitment to social reforms, activist intervention, and belief in non-state, independent volunteer actions – these three principles combined laid the cultural foundation for the Red Cross movement.

A few material and realpolitik conditions helped the realization of such ideas. All the founders were well-connected elites in their professional worlds. Dunant himself was a wealthy businessman with wide connections across Europe. He was also well educated; his dramatic writing in his *Un Souvenir de Solferino* undoubtedly paved the way for the movement. Moynier was involved in about forty charitable organizations. Other founders of the ICRC all enjoyed similar professional prestige and social connections. But these social conditions alone did not turn into an extraordinary humanitarian movement. Many upper-class people in Europe had similar privileges but did not start such a movement. It was the Réveil-inspired moral principles that mattered. The movement's impartiality, independence from political conflicts, and focus on saving lives and reducing suffering were accepted by all the states because the neutral presence of an aid organization might help all sides of the conflicts and set the cultural rules to turn wars from brutal slaughters into rule-governed activities.

When the original model of the Red Cross spread to the rest of the world, it adopted a decentralizing strategy. National Red Cross societies had considerable autonomy to adapt to the norms in their countries. This decentralization structure also came from the Réveil movement, which emphasized the independence of each parish and a loose network of church organizations. An interesting cultural nuance in this process of dissemination was the ICRC's leaders' encouragement of national societies' patriotism in promoting humanitarianism. The ICRC and national Red Cross societies both believed that nationalism and internationalism were compatible with each other.

Nevertheless, the principles of ICRC or humanitarianism in general contain some inevitable tensions. The tensions sometimes lead to moral dilemmas of life and death, which affiliated organizations and workers must face in intense situations. For example, the principles of neutrality and impartiality try to transcend political conflicts without favoring one side or another and to alleviate the suffering of those people who need assistance, regardless of their identities. But the purpose of saving people may not always dovetail with the impartiality principle. For example, if one side in a war commits apparent genocide of the other side, does the ICRC still say and do nothing to prevent the genocide and only devote themselves to caring for the survivors?

The ICRC had to face this tough question in World War II, when their visits to Nazi concentration camps and other alarming reports showed clear evidence of the deportation and killing of Jews. Yet the organization remained silent on the issue, and the files of their World War II involvement were kept confidential until 1996. Their leadership justified their silence by claiming that their impartiality principle was the reason that the ICRC was still admitted by the Nazis to care for the wounded and POWs. If the ICRC had spoken out about the concentration camps, they would have lost access to many other Jews and victims who desperately needed assistance. Consequently, in this painful moral calculus, the ICRC weighed idealism against the greater cost, at the expense of their moral reputation, despite their undoubtedly substantive effort to save lives in the war (Dromi 2020: 119–22).

This dilemma was repeated in later incidents. In the aid operation during the Nigerian Civil War (1967–70), the ICRC negotiated with the Nigerian government to acquire permission to deliver their materials to Biafra, where the Igbos, the ethnic minority group, declared independence and consequently were blockaded by the Nigerian government with an intention to starve the Igbos to death. As the negotiations proved fruitless and each additional day meant more Igbos died, the ICRC decided to act without permission. This uncharacteristic move gave the Nigerian government an excuse to attack the ICRC refugee camp in June 1969. Four French Red Cross aid workers were killed, and an ICRC aircraft carrying provisions was shot down. Except for that brief moment of defiance, however, the ICRC chose not to act without permission from the Nigerian government (Barnett 2011: 137–8). This choice proved highly controversial in an intense conflict and an extreme situation of famine in blockaded Biafra, but alternative decisions seemed equally difficult. In one case, the ICRC instructed their doctors and nurses to leave wounded Biafran villagers who were pursued by the Nigerian army. The doctors disobeyed and stayed, but only to witness the villagers – including children and women – brutally massacred by the Nigerian army.

The slaughter, as well as the ICRC's inaction, appalled and infuriated some Red Cross volunteers, who were also left-wing intellectuals participating in the new social movement in the 1960s. Among them was Bernard Kouchner, then a volunteering physician working for the French Red Cross, who would be the co-founder of Médecins Sans Frontières (MSF, Doctors Without Borders). Kouchner decided to break the code of silence and spoke out in an article in *Le Monde*, calling for international aid for the Biafrans. In stark contrast with the ICRC, MSF represents a new idea of impartiality based on rights and takes a more active role in preventing violence. Yet it is not free from intrinsic tensions. Despite its generally more progressive stance, MSF remains a "cultural basin" of various ideologies, which may be in conflict with each other (Barnett 2011: 145–6). For example, its distinctive concept of *témoignage*, "witnessing," was interpreted by some in MSF as seeing something and saying something: its official website defines *témoignage* as "a willingness to speak on behalf of the people we assist: to bring abuses and intolerable situations to the public eye" (Médecins Sans Frontières 2021). But for many others, it is just seeing without saying.

This tension is general and common in modern humanitarianism. Michael Barnett summarizes it as the tension between *"emergency humanitarianism,"* the action of providing food and shelter, and *"alchemical humanitarianism,"* by which the aid workers also attempt to find the roots of the problems (Barnett 2011: 22). A reader of this book may recall a similar moral dilemma discussed earlier, in local civic engagement, when volunteers are confronted with two options: helping people but keeping quiet on obvious issues; or speaking out about the causes of people's suffering and finding solutions. In humanitarianism, such a dilemma happens at the global level, is embroiled in more complex political and cultural processes, and has much more significant consequences, often life and death for not just a handful but tens of thousands of people. Whatever moral choice the organizations and aid workers make often produces much more emotional stress and more significant consequences than any other situations that have been described in this book.

Such a dilemma was evident in a series of catastrophic events in the 1990s, especially the genocides in Bosnia and Rwanda (Barnett 2011). The failure of the West to intervene in those events made the INGOs involved in the aid work reflect on the downside of the old emergency humanitarianism. To be fair to the INGOs, the failure should mostly be attributed to the Western governments and the intergovernmental organization (IGOs), such as the UN. In Rwanda, the UN ignored early warnings and failed to strengthen its peacekeeping troops to stop the genocide. Later, when INGOs were able to provide aid in the refugee camps along the border of Zaire and Rwanda, aid workers who wanted to speak out were threatened by the Hutu genocidaires who in effect controlled the camps. Adding to the complexity was that most refugees were Hutus, many of whom were encouraged or forced by the government to kill and rape their Tutsi neighbors and fled only when they dreaded being killed by the advancing Rwanda Patriotic Front (the Tutsi rebel army).

In that horrendous situation, even some peacekeeping soldiers were killed. The unarmed INGOs mostly could do nothing and were left to deal with the moral dilemmas by themselves. The horrors in Rwanda and other places in the 1990s, however, have haunted the humanitarian organizations and become a tipping point. After that, most INGOs explicitly adopt a rights-based approach to humanitarianism and put addressing injustice and other root causes of various global problems on their agenda.

Even in relatively peaceful times, the impartiality principle has been confronted with the increasingly complex relationships between INGOs and the states. Many Western states' foreign aid functions have been outsourced to INGOs, and this trend provokes debate over whether INGOs are really independent and impartial or have become part of the general governmentality of the developed countries in controlling and exploiting the global South – as Agier vividly terms it, "the left hand of empire" (Agier 2010). At the very least, many INGOs rely on states for funding and need military protection from states or IGOs like the UN in conflict situations. In other cases, the local state's apparatuses are replaced by Western INGOs; this happened in Haiti, the so-called "republic of NGOs," where the INGOs' lack of coordination and capacity resulted in the chaotic situation in the wake of the 2010 earthquake. In the long run, the ubiquitous presence of INGOs and the seriously weakened Haitian state exacerbate the country's dependence on the West (Dupuy 2010; Zanotti 2010; Edmonds 2012).

Global and Transnational Public Sphere

When Habermas published his *The Structural Transformation of the Public Sphere* in 1962, he could hardly have imagined satellite TV networks and the Internet. Technological advances have made it possible for anyone who has the access and linguistic abilities to know of happenings around the world and to join with people from afar to discuss issues of public concern. International conferences as global public sphere platforms existed long before Habermas – for example, Anti-Slavery International's first world convention, discussed at the beginning of this chapter – but their frequency and scale utterly changed after air travel and communication technologies became convenient. Internet forums function as Habermas's cafés in the twenty-first century, and information technology seems to make his dream come true at a global scale. The *global public sphere*, the new buzzword, has gone well beyond obscure academic books and appeared in the media – giving its name, for example, to Fareed Zacharia's CNN program "GPS (Global Public Sphere)."

Yet the already troubled concept of "public sphere" has even bigger troubles at the global scale. Habermas's original theory covered the emergence and transformation of the public spheres in different European countries, but each public sphere is bound by the territory of a state. In other words, the concept of public sphere is very much within the legal and historical frame of Westphalian sovereignty, which started with the Peace of Westphalia treaties in 1648 and granted each state exclusive sovereignty over its territory. The global public sphere, however, goes beyond the Westphalian frame. Global issues do not stop at the borders of territorial states; an event, such as the COVID-19 pandemic, may happen in different countries; events that happened in one state will be discussed in different parts of the world. Participants in those global discussions do not constitute a political citizenry of a single state.

This global feature of contemporary public spheres poses challenges to Habermas's original theory. Nancy Fraser points out that the essence of Habermas's theory includes two ideas: normative legitimacy (a nation-state's legitimacy relies on citizens' participation in political activities) and political efficacy (whether the public opinion formed in the public sphere can influence the state's political decisions) (Fraser 2007). The two ideas do not make immediate sense in the global context because some significant questions can be raised: legitimacy of *which* state? Efficacy of influence on *which* state? To what extent can we still say the public sphere is a social foundation of democracy if we are not sure which state we are talking about? A potential answer to these questions is "world government!" This idea is not new. Thinkers like Immanuel Kant have argued for such a world polity under which everyone on the planet is a world citizen. Yet none of these cosmopolitan dreams has come true.

In the absence of a world government, the global expansion of the public sphere accentuates and exacerbates some issues that already exist in the Westphalian public spheres, such as social inequality. In the World Anti-Slavery Convention in 1840, the inequality issue was gender discrimination. In other situations, the issue is rather simple: money. To attend an international forum in Davos or Geneva certainly will contribute to the global discourses on pressing issues – as long as you can pay for your trip, or an organization can. In contrast, to attend a *gram sabha* in India, you need only walk to the meeting site. On this matter, a somewhat cynical observation has a point: for some, the global public sphere may be just a fancy name for a VIP club of frequent flyers. To remotely join the global public sphere, one needs at least reliable Internet service, satellite TVs, and electricity, which should not be taken for granted in many countries. To have effective discussions, one needs to master the most commonly used language, English, which, for most people outside the Anglophone sphere is a foreign language. Linguistic ability is highly correlated with educational level, and educational level is highly correlated with socioeconomic status. In a world where an air ticket to a forum in Geneva costs much more than one could earn in a year in many countries, participation in global discourse encounters the same difficulties as in domestic public spheres, but multiplied many times.

Many discussions about the global public sphere happen in the European academic world and its mediated discourses, for good reasons. Contemporary Europe boasts a few features that make a unified, transnational public sphere more possible than in other places: the European Union as its supra-state institutional frame, an internal single market, relatively affluent societies, travel within the EU without visas, many citizens' multilingual abilities, the vibrant media, and, according to Habermas, a tradition of the public sphere. It seems natural to claim that a "European public sphere" exists or at least is coming to exist.

Nevertheless, such a European public sphere was not naturally born after the Maastricht Treaty came into force in 1993. One of the difficulties was conceptual. By what criteria can we say there is a "European public sphere"? One view is of a supranational European public sphere with a single EU-wide media system, and this view quickly proved unrealistic. Another view, therefore, emerged as an alternative, that is, a "transnational European public sphere" with national public spheres as constituents. Two criteria are important for this transnational public sphere: (1) participants in the national public spheres must be mutually aware of the important issues in other national public spheres; (2) participants also must know how people in other national public spheres interpret those issues and the frame in which they debate the issues (Risse 2010).

By these two criteria, some forms of transnational public sphere exist in Europe, but so do gaps between the real and the ideal. Various national media tend to respond to the same EU-wide problems and triggering events, such as the military intervention in Kosovo, and ordinary citizens use the national media to be informed about European issues. Thus, a transnational, European public sphere is at least gradually forming (Kantner 2015). Some studies confirm that the Internet, especially social media, facilitates a European public sphere, but such a sphere is issue-based, limited, and somewhat ad hoc. For example, Max Hänska and Stefan Bauchowitz show that Twitter discussions of the 2015 Greek bailout negotiation and the Eurozone crisis demonstrated clear signs of Europeanization: users interacted with interlocutors in other countries; discussions went well beyond national boundaries; Europeans in various countries shared grievances but held drastically different opinions (Hänska and Bauchowitz 2019). Other than those crisis moments, however, issue-based publics are weak and stratified. Even civil society organizations, particularly those lobbying at the EU level, have only limited intention or capacity to engage in public discussions of global problems such as climate change and fair trade (Bennett et al. 2015).

Findings are less promising about whether ordinary citizens can participate in the transnational public sphere. Jürgen Gerhards and Silke Hans used to two Eurobarometer surveys (in 2007 and 2010, with 500 correspondents in each small country and 1,000 in each bigger country) to investigate whether ordinary citizens' knowledge about key issues of other public spheres met the two criteria mentioned earlier: awareness of issues in other national public spheres and understanding of the interpretations of and debates over the issues (Gerhards and Hans 2014). Their findings may disappoint advocates for a European public sphere: over 90 percent of EU citizens had not read a foreign newspaper in the last twelve months, and nearly 60 percent had not viewed a foreign magazine, book, or TV program. Even those who did consume those cultural products were not necessarily engaging in the debate or aware of the interpretation frameworks in other countries. This general lack of transnational engagement, however, varied across countries: unsurprisingly, those countries with higher educational levels, and thus better language skills, tended to be more transnational. Therefore, social inequality reproduced itself in a transnational public sphere.

All these issues exist and are more serious in other regions in the world. The EU, after all, consists of some of the wealthiest countries, and the disparity among its member states is less than that in the rest of the world. The greater socioeconomic divide between the West and the global South leads to huge gaps in educational level, linguistic ability, and infrastructure for information technology. The gaps also exist in subtler forms. Western media dominate the global public sphere and sometimes treat the South as "other," even as an object of distant suffering or the politics of pity – hungry and desperate children in Africa who show up on Western middle-class families' TVs (Boltanski 1999; Chouliaraki 2013). Even if such images are used for humanitarian purposes, for example, INGOs' use of "provocative" images to raise maximum funds, they may not always show respect for the dignity of the people concerned and have questionable effects on forming a global public sphere with equal and open discussions (Yanacopulos 2016: 76–7). Western audiences tend to shed tears, pour money into an INGO, and then move on with self-congratulations, without any intention to have conversations with the "poor children." Another barrier is political systems. For example, in China, where most people consume domestic media, and foreign media are barred, the state imposes heavy-handed political censorship and even hires citizens to shape – more precisely, to mislead – public opinion about issues in other public spheres (Repnikova and Fang 2018). This type of state-sponsored disinformation campaign has attracted attention from the media but has yet to be effectively studied by cultural sociology.

7

Cultural Sociology as an Art of Listening

In our times, everyone is eager to have their voices heard. It is a valid desire. It is what democracy and civil society are about. Yet a democratic social life also needs a good art of listening. First to understand, next to be understood. To "disagree without being disagreeable," as Ruth Bader Ginsburg, the late US Supreme Court Justice, famously said, one needs to listen to how others talk about themselves and articulate their ideas. Cultural sociology is an "art of listening." Using this analogy, I intend to suggest that "listening" means empirical analysis, whereas "speaking" means expressing normative opinions. The cultural sociology of civil society aims to understand why people engage in public activities, how they talk about the meanings of their actions, and what consequences their thoughts and actions generate in their societies. It is a thoroughly empirical approach that takes people's opinions and ideas seriously but does not impose researchers' own normative judgment on the cases they examine.

To achieve this end, cultural sociology has provided some useful conceptual tools to understand culture and civil society. Cultural sociology, as we have seen, specifies at least four types of culture in civil society: *culture in structure, culture in action, culture in interaction,* and *culture in object.* Here I briefly recapitulate what these conceptual tools have offered us in examining different aspects of civil society (see table 7.1). It is worth reemphasizing that this typological mapping is just analytical; a theory or an empirical study may include more than one concept of culture.

Table 7.1 Concepts and examples of culture in civil society

	Culture in structure	Culture in action	Culture in interaction	Culture in object
The public sphere	Values and codes of mediated discourses	Participants of the public sphere use popular wisdom, personal stories, and emotional expressions to engage in discourses	Speech norms in local conversations, formal deliberation, and mediated discourses	Bookstores that sell library books as counter publics under repressive regimes
Association	Goals and meanings associations pursue	Associations use different items from the culture of democracy to react to particular situations	Norms of interactions among members of associations and groups	N/A
Civic engagement	Internalized values about civic engagement	Individuals mobilize various, often conflicting items in their cultural repertoires to understand and explain their engagement	Norms of interactions and speeches in citizens' engagement	N/A
Global civil society	Culture as a global institution	Culture in international organizations' local practices and moral dilemmas of the humanitarian workers	Speech norms in transnational public spheres.	Reception of cultural meanings in INGOs' campaign aids

Culture in structure. In this notion, culture is defined as structures and classifications of symbols, meanings, and principles, which precede individuals. In studies of the public sphere, Alexander's CST highlights this structural aspect of culture, especially the binary codes that constitute the foundation of civil society (Alexander 2006). Studies of associations do not have a strong structural perspective, but many of them suggest that the goals and meanings that associations pursue are not randomly chosen but are defined in the existing cultural structures. In the literature on civic engagement, despite its analytical unit of individuals, the "civic culture" perspective follows a structural concept of culture because it emphasizes values in the existing political culture internalized by individuals (Almond and Verba 1963). The world culture theory explicitly follows the structural perspective by defining culture as an institution, a global cultural structure with a set of rules and principles that diffuse from the West to the rest of the world (Boli and Thomas 1997).

Culture in action. The "culture in action" perspective emphasizes individuals' agency in picking and choosing different items in the cultural structure to respond to various situations. Many studies of the public sphere show how participants in discourses in the public sphere use popular wisdom, personal stories, and emotional expressions to justify their selective use of cultural and political values. This concept is particularly illuminating in examining how civil society actors – associations and individuals – mobilize various, often conflicting items, such as individualism and various communitarian cultures, in their cultural repertoires to understand and explain their engagement. At the global level, INGOs also selectively use internationally available cultural items to deal with unpredictable local situations, even though such uses often flounder.

Culture in interaction. In this definition, culture means local norms of interactions or styles of communication. In the public sphere, people engaged in various discourses follow speech norms based on specific cultural expectations revolving around the general notion of "civility," including nonviolent, critical, and reasonable ways of communication. The real-world discourses in the public sphere may also contain emotion, drama, and so on. In associational life as well as civic engagement, the interaction norms are often represented in group cultures formed in tiny publics – small groups and associations that connect each other to form networks on which civil society relies. In global civil society, such norms of interactions often appear in the INGOs' practices and their relationships with the local communities and in the transnational public spheres.

Culture in object. Cultural meanings are embodied in tangible objects and the social processes that produce the objects. Although this concept of culture is not widely used in the cultural sociology of civil society, it is occasionally the focus of some valuable studies, for example, the counter-publics that revolve around literary activities and book consumption as well as INGOs' advertisement strategies.

These conceptual tools help us identify the *"culture of democracy"* as the most significant culture in civil society. It is "most significant" not because theorists think it is but because such significance is *real*. The culture of democracy is part of *culture in structure*: a set of values in the cultural structure of modern democracy, such as tolerance, equality, liberty, solidarity, and so on. These values define what an ideal "civil society" is, not only as the goals civil society actors pursue but also as the norms by which civil society actors interact with each other. For example, "equality" is not only a feature of an ideal good society some associations pursue but also the norm of interactions among members of the associations. Nevertheless, the culture of democracy may contain multiple, contradictory cultural items. Moreover, much of the complexity in the culture of democracy comes from the gap between the ideal, structural culture of democracy and its enactment in *actions* and *interactions*. Adding to the complexity is that, in addition to the culture of democracy, other cultures in structure, actions, and interactions may also inform and motivate civil society practices. Thus, cultural sociology addresses variations in and challenges to the culture of democracy in different parts and levels of civil societies.

The theoretical tools of cultural sociology equip us with perspectives and insights to think about many pressing public issues:

effective and democratic public communications, conflicts and solidarity in civil society, political apathy, civil societies under authoritarianism, universal values and local practices, ethical dilemmas in civil society practices, and so on. This book has discussed many examples of how cultural sociologists have analyzed these issues. One thing common to all the analyses, regardless of their theoretical approaches, is that they pay close attention to variations, paradoxes, and dilemmas in real-world civil societies rather than judging reality on some abstract criteria.

To be honest with readers, however, cultural sociology has yet to produce significant studies of a few of the most important issues of civil society in today's world. Take *disinformation* as an example. Disinformation can be defined as "intentional falsehoods or distortions, often spread as news, to advance political goals such as discrediting opponents, disrupting policy debates, influencing voters, inflaming existing social conflicts, or creating a general backdrop of confusion and informational paralysis" (Bennett and Livingston 2021: 3). One does not have much difficulty finding examples of disinformation: online bots that spread rumors about elections, politicians who fabricate numbers and come up with "alternative facts," deniers who attack the scientific evidence for vaccines and climate change, and so on. The current scholarship on disinformation is mostly within political science and communication studies, with a clearly stated assumption that disinformation effectively changes people's minds and thus is responsible for much of the political chaos in Western democracies. These scholars want to find out how and why people would believe in ridiculous and false information.

Cultural sociology could have joined this scholarship. Various approaches to the public sphere could have offered new insights, tested their own theories, and asked new questions. For example, how would CST explain disinformation? Do people still share the same set of binary codes when the information they rely on is completely different? Also, cultural sociologists tend to emphasize people's agency, that is, being able to choose different sources of information. But does this argument about agency still hold when the existing scholarship and our everyday observations already show that people are much more susceptible than expected to disinformation? Or, if we still believe in the agency argument, can we say the power of disinformation comes from agency itself, that is, to pick or "consume" the rumors or conspiracy theories you like but avoid the ones you dislike? If so, are we sociologists walking in a circle by going back to the "mass society" argument or the Frankfurt School's "culture industry" argument that seemingly autonomous individuals are in fact gullible consumers of manufactured information? All these questions could be a starting point for future research in the cultural sociology of civil society.

Cultural sociology is certainly not a panacea for all the problems we are facing now. No social science can be a panacea. Cultural sociology, however, has a strong potential to raise and answer important questions. Cultural sociology does not provide us with normative judgments; rather, it provides empirical observations for us to think about the reasons and consequences of our judgements. Its analytical strength comes from its postulate that culture informs, encourages, motivates, and regulates people who take actions to improve society. It is in this empirical sense that culture is the very "soul" of civil society.

References

Adorno, T. W., Frenkel-Brunswik, E., Levinson, D. J., & Sanford, R. N. (1950) *The Authoritarian Personality*. New York, NY: Harper.

Agier, M. (2010) Humanity as an Identity and Its Political Effects: A Note on Camps and Humanitarian Government. *Humanity*, 1: 29–45.

Alexander, J. C. (2006) *The Civil Sphere*, Oxford, UK, and New York, NY: Oxford University Press.

Alexander, J. C. (2021) Introduction. *In:* Alexander, J. C., Kivisto, P., & Sciortino, G. (eds.) *Populism in the Civil Sphere*. Cambridge, UK: Polity.

Alexander, J. C., Kivisto, P., & Sciortino, G. (eds.) (2021) *Populism in the Civil Sphere*, Cambridge, UK: Polity.

Alexander, J. C., Palmer, D. A., Park, S., & Ku, A. S.-M. (eds.) (2019) *The Civil Sphere in East Asia*, Cambridge, UK: Cambridge University Press.

Alexander, J. C. & Smith, P. (1993) The Discourse of American Civil Society: A New Proposal for Cultural Studies. *Theory and Society*, 22: 151–207.

Alexander, J. C., Stack, T., & Khosrokhavar, F. (eds.) (2020) *Breaching the Civil Order: Radicalism and the Civil Sphere*, Cambridge, UK, and New York, NY: Cambridge University Press.

Alexander, J. C. & Tognato, C. (eds.) (2018) *The Civil Sphere in Latin America*, Cambridge, UK: Cambridge University Press.

Allport, G. W. (1954) *The Nature of Prejudice*, Cambridge, MA: Addison-Wesley.

Almond, G. A. & Verba, S. (1963) *The Civic Culture: Political Attitudes and Democracy in Five Nations*, Princeton, NJ: Princeton University Press.

Arato, A. (1981) Civil Society Against the State: Poland 1980–81. *Telos*, 1981: 23–47.

Arato, A. & Cohen, J. L. (2017) Civil Society, Populism and Religion. *Constellations*, 24: 283–95.

Arendt, H. (1968) *The Origins of Totalitarianism*, New York, NY: Harvest.

References

Armony, A. C. (2004) *The Dubious Link: Civic Engagement and Democratization*, Stanford, CA: Stanford University Press.

Bail, C. (2015) *Terrified: How Anti-Muslim Fringe Organizations Became Mainstream*, Princeton, NJ: Princeton University Press.

Bail, C. (2021) *Breaking the Social Media Prism: How to Make Our Platforms Less Polarizing*, Princeton, NJ, and Oxford, UK: Princeton University Press.

Bail, C. A., Brown, T. W., & Mann, M. (2017) Channeling Hearts and Minds: Advocacy Organizations, Cognitive-Emotional Currents, and Public Conversation. *American Sociological Review*, 82: 1188–1213.

Baiocchi, G. (2003) Emergent Public Spheres: Talking Politics in Participatory Governance. *American Sociological Review*, 68: 52–74.

Baiocchi, G. (2005) *Miltants and Citizens: The Politics of Participatory Democracy in Porto Alegre*, Stanford, CA: Stanford University Press.

Baiocchi, G. (2006) The Civilizing Force of Social Movements: Corporate and Liberal Codes in Brazil's Public Sphere. *Sociological Theory*, 24: 285–311.

Baiocchi, G. (2013) *The Civic Imagination: Making a Difference in American Political Life*, Boulder, CO: Paradigm.

Barbalet, J. M. (2002) *Emotions and Sociology*, Oxford, UK, and Malden, MA: Blackwell/Socological Review.

Barberá, P., Jost, J. T., Nagler, J., Tucker, J. A., & Bonneau, R. (2015) Tweeting from Left to Right: Is Online Political Communication More Than an Echo Chamber? *Psychological Science*, 26: 1531–42.

Barnett, M. N. (2011) *Empire of Humanity: A History of Humanitarianism*, Ithaca, NY: Cornell University Press.

Barrett, M. & Pachi, D. (2019) *Youth Civic and Political Engagement*, London, UK, and New York, NY: Routledge.

Bellah, R. N., Madsen, R., Sullivan, W. M., Swidler, A., & Tipton, S. M. ([1985] 2008) *Habits of the Heart: Individualism and Commitment in American Life*, Berkeley, CA: University of California Press.

Bennett, E. A., Cordner, A., Klein, P. T., Savell, S., & Baiocchi, G. (2013) Disavowing Politics: Civic Engagement in an Era of Political Skepticism. *American Journal of Sociology*, 119: 518–48.

Bennett, W. L., Lang, S., & Segerberg, A. (2015) European Issue Publics Online: The Cases of Climate Change and Fair Trade. *In:* Risse, T. (ed.) *European Public Spheres: Politics Is Back*. Cambridge, UK: Cambridge University Press.

Bennett, W. L. & Livingston, S. (2021) A Brief History of the Disinformation Age: Information Wars and the Decline of Institutional Authority. *In:* Bennett, W. L. & Livingston, S. (eds.) *The Disinformation Age: Politics, Technology, and Disruptive Communication in the United States*. New York, NY: Cambridge University Press.

Berger, B. (2009) Political Theory, Political Science, and the End of Civic Engagement. *Perspectives on Politics*, 7: 335–49.

References

Berman, S. (1997) Civil Society and the Collapse of the Weimar Republic. *World Politics*, 49: 401–29.

Bernhard, M. H. (1993) *The Origins of Democratization in Poland: Workers, Intellectuals and Oppositional Politics, 1976–1980*, New York, NY: Columbia University Press.

Beyerlein, K. & Sikkink, D. (2008) Sorrow and Solidarity: Why Americans Volunteered for 9/11 Relief Efforts. *Social Problems*, 55: 190–215.

Beyerlein, K. & Vaisey, S. (2013) Individualism Revisited: Moral Worldviews and Civic Engagement. *Poetics*, 41: 384–406.

Blee, K. M. (2012) *Democracy in the Making: How Activist Groups Form*, Oxford, UK, and New York, NY: Oxford University Press.

Bloemraad, I. & Terriquez, V. (2016) Cultures of Engagement: The Organizational Foundations of Advancing Health in Immigrant and Low-Income Communities of Color. *Social Science & Medicine*, 165: 214–22.

Boli, J., Loya, T. A., & Loftin, T. (1999) National Participation in World-Polity Organization. *In*: Boli, J. & Thomas, G. M. (eds.) *Constructing World Culture: International Nongovernmental Organizations Since 1875*. Stanford, CA: Stanford University Press.

Boli, J. & Thomas, G. M. (1997) World Culture in the World Polity: A Century of International Non-Governmental Organization. *American Sociological Review*, 62: 171–90.

Boltanski, L. (1999) *Distant Suffering: Morality, Media, and Politics*, Cambridge, UK, and New York, NY: Cambridge University Press.

Botello, N. A. & Magnoni, J. A. (2018) The Civil Sphere in Mexico: Between Democracy and Authoritarianism. *In*: Alexander, J. C. & Tognato, C. (eds.) *The Civil Sphere in Latin America*. Cambridge, UK: Cambridge University Press.

Bourdieu, P. & Wacquant, L. (2013) Symbolic Capital and Social Classes. *Journal of Classical Sociology*, 13: 292–302.

Braunstein, R. (2017) *Prophets and Patriots: Faith in Democracy across the Political Divide*, Oakland, CA: University of California Press.

Bromley, P., Schofer, E., & Longhofer, W. (2020) Contentions over World Culture: The Rise of Legal Restrictions on Foreign Funding to NGOs, 1994–2015. *Social Forces*, 99: 281–304.

Brook, T. & Frolic, B. M. (eds.) (1997) *Civil Society in China*, Armonk, NY: M. E. Sharpe.

Brubaker, R. (2017) Why Populism? *Theory and Society*, 46: 357–85.

Bryan, F. M. (2004) *Real Democracy: The New England Town Meeting and How It Works*, Chicago, IL, and London, UK: University of Chicago Press.

Burke, K. (1945) *A Grammar of Motives*, New York, NY: Prentice Hall.

Burnet, J. E. (2008) Gender Balance and the Meanings of Women in Governance in Post-Genocide Rwanda. *African Affairs*, 107: 361–86.

Büyükokutan, B. (2018) Elitist by Default? Interaction Dynamics and the

References

Inclusiveness of Secularization in Turkish Literary Milieus. *American Journal of Sociology*, 123: 1249–95.

Calhoun, C. J. (ed.) (1992) *Habermas and the Public Sphere*, Cambridge, MA: MIT Press.

Calhoun, C. J. (1994) *Neither Gods Nor Emperors: Students and the Struggle for Democracy in China*, Berkeley, CA: University of California Press.

Carothers, T. & Brechenmacher, S. (2014) *Closing Space: Democracy and Human Rights Support Under Fire*, Washington, DC: Carnegie Endowment for International Peace.

Cavatorta, F. (ed.) (2013) *Civil Society Activism under Authoritarian Rule: A Comparative Perspective*, London, UK, and New York, NY: Routledge.

Chan, K.-M. (2020) *Chan Kin-man's Letters from Prison*, Hong Kong: Step Forward Multimedia.

Chouliaraki, L. (2013) *The Ironic Spectator: Solidarity in the Age of Post-Humanitarianism*, Cambridge, UK, and Malden, MA: Polity.

Christensen, D. & Weinstein, J. M. (2013) Defunding Dissent: Restrictions on Aid to NGOs. *Journal of Democracy*, 24: 77–91.

Clemens, E. S. (2020) *Civic Gifts: Voluntarism and the Making of the American Nation-State*, Chicago, IL: University of Chicago Press.

Collins, R. (2004) Rituals of Solidarity and Security in the Wake of Terrorist Attack. *Sociological Theory*, 22: 53–87.

Compion, S., Cnaan, R. A., Brudney, J. L., Jeong, B. G., Zhang, C., & Haski-Leventhal, D. (2021) "Young, Fun, and Free": Episodic Volunteers in Ghana, South Africa and Tanzania. *Voluntas* [Online]. Available:. https://doi.org/10.1007/s11266-021-00324-y

Conover, P. J., Searing, D. D., & Crewe, I. M. (2002) The Deliberative Potential of Political Discussion. *British Journal of Political Science*, 32: 21–62.

Cramer, K. J. (2016) *The Politics of Resentment: Rural Consciousness in Wisconsin and the Rise of Scott Walker*, Chicago, IL: University of Chicago Press.

De Santos, M. (2009) Fact-Totems and the Statistical Imagination: The Public Life of a Statistic in Argentina 2001. *Sociological Theory*, 27: 466–89.

Dewey, J. (1916) *Democracy and Education: An Introduction to the Philosophy of Education*, New York, NY: Macmillan.

Dodge, J. & Ospina, S. M. (2016) Nonprofits as "Schools of Democracy": A Comparative Case Study of Two Environmental Organizations. *Nonprofit and Voluntary Sector Quarterly*, 45: 478–99.

Dromi, S. M. (2020) *Above the Fray: The Red Cross and the Making of the Humanitarian Sector*, Chicago, IL, and London, UK: University of Chicago Press.

Dupuy, A. (2010) *Beyond the Earthquake: A Wake-Up Call for Haiti* [Online]. Available: http://www.ssrc.org/features/pages/haiti-now-and-next/1338/1339.

Durkheim, E. (1933) *The Division of Labor in Society*, Glencoe, IL: Free Press.

References

Durkheim, E. ([1912] 1995) *The Elementary Forms of Religious Life*, New York, NY: Free Press.

Economist (2014) Donors: Keep Out; Foreign Funding of NGOs. *The Economist*.

Economist Intelligence Unit (2021) *Democracy Index 2020: In Sickness and in Health?* [Online] Available: https://www.eiu.com/n/campaigns/democracy-index-2020/?utm_source=economist-daily-chart&utm_medium=anchor&utm_campaign=democracy-index-2020&utm_content=anchor-1.

Edgell, P., Hull, K. E., Green, K., & Winchester, D. (2016) Reasoning Together Through Telling Stories: How People Talk about Social Controversies. *Qualitative Sociology*, 39: 1–26.

Edmonds, K. (2012) Beyond Good Intentions: The Structural Limitations of NGOs in Haiti. *Critical Sociology*, 39: 439–52.

Edwards, B., Foley, M. W., & Diani, M. (eds.) (2001) *Beyond Tocqueville: Civil Society and the Social Capital Debate in Comparative Perspective*, Hanover, NH: University Press of New England.

Edwards, M. (2020) *Civil Society*, Cambridge, UK, and Malden, MA: Polity.

Ehrenberg, J. (2017) *Civil Society: The Critical History of an Idea*, New York, NY: New York University Press.

Ekiert, G. & Kubik, J. (2014) The Legacies of 1989: Myths and Realities of Civil Society. *Journal of Democracy*, 25: 46–58.

Eliasoph, N. (1998) *Avoiding Politics: How Americans Produce Apathy in Everyday Life*, Cambridge, UK, and New York, NY: Cambridge University Press.

Eliasoph, N. (2011) *Making Volunteers: Civic Life after Welfare's End*, Princeton, NJ, and Oxford, UK: Princeton University Press.

Eliasoph, N. & Lichterman, P. (2003) Culture in Interaction. *American Journal of Sociology*, 108: 735–94.

Emirbayer, M. & Sheller, M. (1999) Publics in History. *Theory and Society*, 28: 145–97.

Erdurmazlı, E. (2019) Satisfaction and Commitment in Voluntary Organizations: A Cultural Analysis Along with Servant Leadership. *Voluntas*, 30: 129–46.

Ferree, M. M., Gamson, W. A., Gerhards, J., & Rucht, D. (2002a) Four Models of the Public Sphere in Modern Democracies. *Theory and Society*, 31: 289–324.

Ferree, M. M., Gamson, W. A., Gerhards, J., & Rucht, D. (2002b) *Shaping Abortion Discourse: Democracy and the Public Sphere in Germany and the United States*, Cambridge, UK: Cambridge University Press.

Fine, G. A. (1987) *With the Boys: Little League Baseball and Preadolescent Culture*, Chicago, IL, and London, UK: University of Chicago Press.

Fine, G. A. (2012) Group Culture and the Interaction Order: Local Sociology on the Meso-Level. *Annual Review of Sociology*, 38: 159–79.

Fine, G. A. (2021) *The Hinge: Civil Society, Group Cultures, and the Power of Local Commitments*, Chicago, IL: University of Chicago Press.

References

Finnemore, M. (1999) Rules of War and Wars of Rules: The International Red Cross and the Restraint of State Violence. *In:* Boli, J. & Thomas, G. M. (eds.) *Constructing World Culture: International Nongovernmental Organizations Since 1875.* Stanford, CA: Stanford University Press.

Fiorina, M. P. (1999) Extreme Voices: A Dark Side of Civic Engagement. *In:* Skocpol, T. & Fiorina, M. P. (eds.) *Civic Engagement in American Democracy.* Washington, DC, and New York, NY: Brookings Institution Press/Russell Sage Foundation.

Fishkin, J. S. (2009) *When People Speak: Deliberative Democracy and Public Consultation,* Oxford, UK, and New York, NY: Oxford University Press.

Frank, D. J., Hironaka, A., & Schofer, E. (2000) The Nation-State and the Natural Environment over the Twentieth Century. *American Sociological Review,* 65: 96–116.

Frank, D. J., Longhofer, W., & Schofer, E. (2007) World Society, NGOs and Environmental Policy Reform in Asia. *International Journal of Comparative Sociology,* 48: 275–95.

Fraser, N. (1992) Rethinking the Public Sphere: A Contribution to the Critique of Actually Existing Democracy. *In:* Calhoun, C. J. (ed.) *Habermas and the Public Sphere,* Cambridge, MA: MIT Press.

Fraser, N. (2007) Special Section: Transnational Public Sphere: Transnationalizing the Public Sphere: On the Legitimacy and Efficacy of Public Opinion in a Post-Westphalian World. *Theory, Culture & Society,* 24: 7–30.

Gamson, W. A. (1992) *Talking Politics,* Cambridge, UK: Cambridge University Press.

Gerhards, J. R. & Hans, S. (2014) Explaining Citizens' Participation in a Transnational European Public Sphere. *Comparative Sociology,* 13: 667–91.

Gerteis, J. (2002) The Possession of Civic Virtue: Movement Narratives of Race and Class in the Knights of Labor. *American Journal of Sociology,* 108: 580–615.

Getler, M. (1978) History Is Uncensored in Poland's "Flying Universities." *The Washington Post,* July 5.

Goffman, E. (1959) *The Presentation of Self in Everyday Life,* Garden City, NY: Doubleday.

Goffman, E. (1983) The Interaction Order. *American Sociological Review,* 48: 1–17.

Goldfarb, J. C. (2006) *The Politics of Small Things: The Power of the Powerless in Dark Times,* Chicago, IL: University of Chicago Press.

Griswold, W. (2013) *Cultures and Societies in a Changing World,* Thousand Oaks, CA: SAGE.

Gusfield, J. R. (1981) *The Culture of Public Problems: Drinking-Driving and the Symbolic Order,* Chicago, IL: University of Chicago Press.

Gutmann, A. & Thompson, D. (2004) *Why Deliberative Democracy?,* Princeton, NJ, and Oxford, UK: Princeton University Press.

References

Habermas, J. (1989) *The Structural Transformation of the Public Sphere: An Inquiry into a Category of Bourgeois Society*, Cambridge, MA: MIT Press.

Haddad, M. A. (2007) *Politics and Volunteering in Japan: A Global Perspective*, Cambridge, UK, and New York, NY: Cambridge University Press.

Haddad, M. A. (2012) *Building Democracy in Japan*, Cambridge, UK, and New York, NY: Cambridge University Press.

Haerpfer, C. W., Bernhagen, P., Welzel, C., & Inglehart, R. F. (eds.) (2019) *Democratization*, Oxford, UK: Oxford University Press.

Hafner-Burton, E. M. & Tsutsui, K. (2005) Human Rights in a Globalizing World: The Paradox of Empty Promises. *American Journal of Sociology*, 110: 1373–1411.

Hall, J. A. (1995) In Search of Civil Society. *In:* Hall, J. A. (ed.) *Civil Society: Theory, History, Comparison*. Cambridge, UK: Polity.

Hänska, M. & Bauchowitz, S. (2019) Can Social Media Facilitate a European Public Sphere?: Transnational Communication and the Europeanization of Twitter During the Eurozone Crisis. *Social Media + Society*, 2019: 1–14.

Havel, V. (1985) *The Power of the Powerless: Citizens Against the State in Central-Eastern Europe*, London, UK, and New York, NY: Routledge.

Held, D. (2006) *Models of Democracy*, Stanford, CA: Stanford University Press.

Hibbing, J. R. & Theiss-Morse, E. (2002) *Stealth Democracy: Americans' Beliefs about How Government Should Work*, Cambridge, UK: Cambridge University Press.

Hildebrandt, T. (2013) *Social Organizations and the Authoritarian State in China*, Cambridge, UK, and New York, NY: Cambridge University Press.

Hobsbawm, E. J. & Ranger, T. O. (eds.) (1983) *The Invention of Tradition*, Cambridge, UK, and New York, NY: Cambridge University Press.

Hochschild, A. R. (2018) *Strangers in Their Own Land: Anger and Mourning on the American Right*, New York, NY: New Press.

Hooghe, M. (2003) Value Congruence and Convergence Within Voluntary Associations: Ethnocentrism in Belgian Organizations. *Political Behavior*, 25: 151–75.

Horvath, A. (2020) The Transformative Potential of Experience: Learning, Group Dynamics, and the Development of Civic Virtue in a Mobile Soup Kitchen. *Voluntas*, 31: 981–94.

Hsu, C., Chen, F.-Y., Horsley, J. P., & Stern, R. (2016) *The State of NGOs in China Today* [Online]. Available: https://www.brookings.edu/blog/up-front/2016/12/15/the-state-of-ngos-in-china-today.

Hsu, J. Y. J. (2017) *State of Exchange: Migrant NGOs and the Chinese Government*, Vancouver and Toronto, Canada: UBC Press.

Hu, M., Guo, C., & Bies, A. (2016) Termination of Nonprofit Alliances: Evidence from China. *Voluntas*, 27: 2490–513.

Huntington, S. P. (1991) *The Third Wave: Democratization in the Late Twentieth Century*, Norman, OK: University of Oklahoma Press.

References

Jacobs, R. N. (1996) Civil Society and Crisis: Culture, Discourse, and the Rodney King Beating. *American Journal of Sociology*, 101: 1238–72.

Jamal, A. A. (2007) *Barriers to Democracy: The Other Side of Social Capital in Palestine and the Arab World*, Princeton, NJ, and Oxford, UK: Princeton University Press.

Jasper, J. M. (2014) *Protest: A Cultural Introduction to Social Movement*, Cambridge, UK: Polity.

Junker, A. (2019) *Becoming Activists in Global China: Social Movements in the Chinese Diaspora*, Cambridge, UK: Cambridge University Press.

Junker, A. & Chan, C. (2019) Fault Line in the Civil Sphere: Explaining New Divisions in Hong Kong's Opposition Movement. *In:* Alexander, J. C., Palmer, D. A., Park, S., & Ku, A. S.-M. (eds.) *The Civil Sphere in East Asia.* Cambridge, UK: Cambridge University Press.

Kaldor, M. (2003) *Global Civil Society: An Answer to War.* Cambridge, UK: Polity.

Kang, X. & Han, H. (2008) Graduated Controls: The State–Society Relationship in Contemporary China. *Modern China*, 34: 36–55.

Kantner, C. (2015) National Media as Transnational Discourse Arenas: The Case of Humanitarian Military Intervention. *In:* Risse, T. (ed.) *European Public Spheres: Politics Is Back.* Cambridge, UK: Cambridge University Press.

Kaufman, J. (2002) *For the Common Good? American Civic Life and the Golden Age of Fraternity*, Oxford, UK, and New York, NY: Oxford University Press.

Keane, J. (1988) *Civil Society and the State: New European Perspectives*, London, UK, and New York, NY: Verso.

Keane, J. (1998) *Civil Society: Old Images, New Visions*, Stanford, CA: Stanford University Press.

Keane, J. (2009) *The Life and Death of Democracy*, London, UK: Pocket Books.

Kemp-Welch, A. (2008) *Poland Under Communism: A Cold War History*, Cambridge, UK, and New York, NY: Cambridge University Press.

Kennedy, M. D. (1991) *Professionals, Power, and Solidarity in Poland: A Critical Sociology of Soviet-Type Society*, Cambridge, UK, and New York, NY: Cambridge University Press.

Kennedy, M. D. (2002) *Cultural Formations of Postcommunism: Emancipation, Transition, Nation, and War*, Minneapolis, MN, and London, UK: University of Minnesota Press.

Kew, D. (2016) *Civil Society, Conflict Resolution, and Democracy in Nigeria*, Syracuse, NY: Syracuse University Press.

Kim, S. (2000) *The Politics of Democratization in Korea: The Role of Civil Society*, Pittsburgh, PA: University of Pittsburgh Press.

Ku, A. S.-M. (2019) Performing Civil Disobedience in Hong Kong. *In:* Alexander, J. C., Palmer, D. A., Park, S., & Ku, A. S.-M. (eds.) *The Civil Sphere in East Asia.* Cambridge, UK: Cambridge University Press.

Kubik, J. (1994) *The Power of Symbols Against the Symbols of Power: The Rise*

References

of Solidarity and the Fall of State Socialism in Poland, University Park, PA: Pennsylvania State University Press.

Kumar, K. (1993) Civil Society: An Inquiry into the Usefulness of an Historical Term. *British Journal of Sociology*, 44: 375–95.

Kwon, H.-K. (2004) Associations, Civic Norms, and Democracy: Revisiting the Italian Case. *Theory and Society*, 33: 135–66.

Langohr, V. (2004) Too Much Civil Society, Too Little Politics: Egypt and Liberalizing Arab Regimes. *Comparative Politics*, 36: 181–204.

Lasswell, H. D. (1951) *The Political Writings of Harold D. Lasswell*, Glencoe, IL: Free Press.

Lechner, F. J. & Boli, J. (2005) *World Culture: Origins and Consequences*, Malden, MA, and Oxford, UK: Blackwell.

Lewis, D. (2013) Civil Society and the Authoritarian State: Cooperation, Contestation and Discourse. *Journal of Civil Society*, 9: 325–40.

Lichterman, P. (1996) *The Search for Political Community: American Activists Reinventing Commitment*, Cambridge, UK, and New York, NY: Cambridge University Press.

Lichterman, P. (2005) Civic Culture at the Grass Roots. *In:* Jacobs, M. D. & Hanrahan, N. W. (eds.) *The Blackwell Companion to the Sociology of Culture.* Oxford, UK: Blackwell.

Lichterman, P. & Eliasoph, N. (2014) Civic Action. *American Journal of Sociology*, 120: 798–863.

Linz, J. J. & Stepan, A. C. (1996) *Problems of Democratic Transition and Consolidation: Southern Europe, South America, and Post-Communist Europe*, Baltimore, MD: Johns Hopkins University Press.

Lo, M.-C. (2010) Cultures of Democracy: A Civil-Society Approach. *In:* Hall, J. R., Grindstaff, L., & Lo, M.-C. (eds.) *Handbook of Cultural Sociology.* New York, NY: Routledge.

Lo, M.-C. M. & Bettinger, C. P. (2009) Civic Solidarity in Hong Kong and Taiwan. *The China Quarterly*, 197: 183–203.

Lo, M.-C. M. & Fan, Y. (2010) Hybrid Cultural Codes in Nonwestern Civil Society: Images of Women in Taiwan and Hong Kong. *Sociological Theory*, 28: 167–92.

Lo, M.-C. M. & Otis, E. M. (2003) Guanxi Civility: Processes, Potentials, and Contingencies. *Politics & Society*, 31: 131–62.

Madsen, R. (1998) *China's Catholics: Tragedy and Hope in an Emerging Civil Society*, Berkeley, CA: University of California Press.

Mansbridge, J. J. (1983) *Beyond Adversary Democracy*, Chicago, IL, and London, UK: University of Chicago Press.

Maynard, D. H. (1960) The World's Anti-Slavery Convention of 1840. *The Mississippi Valley Historical Review*, 47: 452–71.

McDonnell, T. E. (2016) *Best Laid Plans: Cultural Entropy and the Unraveling of AIDS Media Campaigns*, Chicago, IL: University of Chicago Press.

References

McPherson, M., Smith-Lovin, L., & Cook, J. M. (2001) Birds of a Feather: Homophily in Social Networks. *Annual Review of Sociology*, 27: 415–44.

Médecins Sans Frontières. (2021) *Advocacy and Témoignage* [Online]. Available: https://msf.org.au/advocacy-and-t%C3%A9moignage.

Meyer, J. W., Boli, J., Thomas, G. M., & Ramirez, F. O. (1997) World Society and the Nation-State. *American Journal of Sociology*, 103: 144–81.

Meyer, J. W., Krücken, G., & Drori, G. S. (2009) *World Society: The Writings of John W. Meyer*, Oxford, UK, and New York, NY: Oxford University Press.

Mill, J. S. (1848) *Principles of Political Economy with Some of Their Applications to Social Philosophy*, London, UK: John W. Parker, West Strand.

Ministry of Civil Affairs of People's Republic of China. (2019) *National Social Service Statistics of the 4th Quarter of 2018* [Online]. Available: http://www.mca.gov.cn/article/sj/tjjb/qgsj/2018/20181201301328.html.

Müller, J.-W. (2016) *What Is Populism?*, Philadelphia, PA: University of Pennsylvania Press.

Mutz, D. C. (2002) Cross-Cutting Social Networks: Testing Democratic Theory in Practice. *American Political Science Review*, 96: 111–26.

Newton, K. (2001) Social Capital and Democracy. *In*: Edwards, B., Foley, M. W., & Diani, M. (eds.) *Beyond Tocqueville: Civil Society and the Social Capital Debate in Comparative Perspective*. Hanover, NH: University Press of New England.

Ning, R. & Palmer, D. A. (2020) Ethics of the Heart: Moral Breakdown and the Aporia of Chinese Volunteers. *Current Anthropology*, 61: 395–417.

Norris, P. & Inglehart, R. (2019) *Cultural Backlash: Trump, Brexit, and Authoritarian Populism*, New York, NY: Cambridge University Press.

Norwegian Nobel Institute. (2015) *2015 National Dialogue Quartet Tunisia* [Online]. Available: https://www.nobelpeaceprize.org/Prize-winners/Winners/2015.

Ost, D. (1990) *Solidarity and the Politics of Anti-Politics: Opposition and Reform in Poland Since 1968*, Philadelphia, PA: Temple University Press.

Ost, D. (2005) *The Defeat of Solidarity: Anger and Politics in Postcommunist Europe*, Ithaca, NY: Cornell University Press.

Palmer, D. A. & Alexander, J. C. (2019) Introduction: The Civil Sphere in the Cultural and Political Transformations of Modern East Asia. *In*: Alexander, J. C., Palmer, D. A., Park, S., & Ku, A. S.-M. (eds.) *The Civil Sphere in East Asia*. Cambridge, UK: Cambridge University Press.

Parthasarathy, R. & Rao, V. (2018) Deliberative Democracy in India. *In*: Bächtiger, A., Dryzek, J. S., Mansbridge, J., & Warren, M. (eds.) *The Oxford Handbook of Deliberative Democracy*. Oxford, UK: Oxford University Press.

Parthasarathy, R., Rao, V., & Palaniswamy, N. (2019) Deliberative Democracy in an Unequal World: A Text-as-Data Study of South India's Village Assemblies. *American Political Science Review*, 113: 623–40.

References

Perrin, A. J. (2006) *Citizen Speak: The Democratic Imagination in American Life*, Chicago, IL: University of Chicago Press.

Perrin, A. J. & Vaisey, S. (2008) Parallel Public Spheres: Distance and Discourse in Letters to the Editor. *American Journal of Sociology*, 114: 781–810.

Peterson, R. A. & Anand, N. (2004) The Production of Culture Perspective. *Annual Review of Sociology*, 30: 311–34.

Polletta, F. (2020) *Inventing the Ties that Bind: Imagined Relationships in Moral and Political Life*, Chicago, IL, and London, UK: University of Chicago Press.

Polletta, F. & Chen, P. C. B. (2013) Gender and Public Talk: Accounting for Women's Variable Participation in the Public Sphere. *Sociological Theory*, 31: 291–317.

Polletta, F. & Lee, J. (2006) Is Telling Stories Good for Democracy? Rhetoric in Public Deliberation after 9/11. *American Sociological Review*, 71: 699–723.

Putnam, R. D. (2000) *Bowling Alone: The Collapse and Revival of American Community*, New York, NY: Simon & Schuster.

Putnam, R. D. (ed.) (2002) *Democracies in Flux: The Evolution of Social Capital in Contemporary Society*, Oxford, UK, and New York, NY: Oxford University Press.

Putnam, R. D., Leonardi, R., & Nanetti, R. (1993) *Making Democracy Work: Civic Traditions in Modern Italy*, Princeton, NJ: Princeton University Press.

Rabinovitch, E. (2001) Gender and the Public Sphere: Alternative Forms of Integration in Nineteenth-Century America. *Sociological Theory*, 19: 344–70.

Rao, V. & Sanyal, P. (2010) Dignity Through Discourse: Poverty and the Culture of Deliberation in Indian Village Democracies. *The Annals of the American Academy of Political and Social Science*, 629: 146–72.

Repnikova, M. & Fang, K. (2018) Authoritarian Participatory Persuasion 2.0: Netizens as Thought Work Collaborators in China. *Journal of Contemporary China*, 27: 763–79.

Riley, D. (2005) Civic Associations and Authoritarian Regimes in Interwar Europe: Italy and Spain in Comparative Perspective. *American Sociological Review*, 70: 288–310.

Risse, T. (2010) *A Community of Europeans? Transnational Identities and Public Spheres*, Ithaca, NY: Cornell University Press.

Roggeband, C. & Glasius, M. (2020) Uncivil Society. *In*: List, R. A., Anheier, H. K., & Toepler, S. (eds.) *International Encyclopedia of Civil Society*. New York, NY: Springer.

Ryfe, D. M. (2006) Narrative and Deliberation in Small Group Forums. *Journal of Applied Communication Research*, 34: 72–93.

Schechner, R. (2002) *Performance Studies: An Introduction*, London, UK, and New York, NY: Routledge.

Schleifer, J. T. (2012) *The Chicago Companion to Tocqueville's Democracy in America*, Chicago, IL: University of Chicago Press.

References

Schnable, A. (2021) *Amateurs Without Borders: The Aspirations and Limits of Global Compassion*, Oakland, CA: University of California Press.

Schudson, M. (1997) Why Conversation Is Not the Soul of Democracy. *Critical Studies in Mass Communication*, 14: 297–309.

Schwadel, P. (2002) Testing the Promise of the Churches: Income Inequality in the Opportunity to Learn Civic Skills in Christian Congregations. *Journal for the Scientific Study of Religion*, 41: 565–75.

Scott, J. C. (1972) Patron–Client Politics and Political Change in Southeast Asia. *American Political Science Review*, 66: 91–113.

Seligman, A. B. (1995) *The Idea of Civil Society*, Princeton, NJ: Princeton University Press.

Sewell, W. H., Jr. (1999) The Concept(s) of Culture. In: Bonnell, V. E., Hunt, L., & Biernacki, R. (eds.) *Beyond the Cultural Turn: New Directions in the Study of Society and Culture*. Berkeley, CA: University of California Press.

Shils, E. (1997) *The Virtue of Civility: Selected Essays on Liberalism, Tradition, and Civil Society*, Indianapolis, IN: Liberty Fund.

Skocpol, T. & Williamson, V. (2012) *The Tea Party and the Remaking of Republican Conservatism*, Oxford, UK, and New York, NY: Oxford University Presss.

Smith, P. & Howe, N. (2015) *Climate Change as Social Drama: Global Warming in the Public Sphere*, Cambridge, UK: Cambridge University Press.

Solórzano, D. G. & Yosso, T. J. (2002) Critical Race Methodology: Counter-Storytelling as an Analytical Framework for Education Research. *Qualitative Inquiry*, 8: 23–44.

Spires, A. J. (2011) Contingent Symbiosis and Civil Society in an Authoritarian State: Understanding the Survival of China's Grassroots NGOs. *American Journal of Sociology*, 117: 1–45.

Spires, A. J. (2018) Chinese Youth and Alternative Narratives of Volunteering. *China Information*, 32: 203–23.

Stern, R. E. & Hassid, J. (2012) Amplifying Silence: Uncertainty and Control Parables in Contemporary China. *Comparative Political Studies*, 45: 1230–54.

Stern, R. E. & O'Brien, K. J. (2012) Politics at the Boundary: Mixed Signals and the Chinese State. *Modern China*, 38: 174–98.

Swidler, A. (1986) Culture in Action: Symbols and Strategies. *American Sociological Review*, 51: 273–86.

Swidler, A. (2001) *Talk of Love: How Culture Matters*, Chicago, IL: University of Chicago Press.

Swidler, A. & Watkins, S. C. (2017) *A Fraught Embrace: The Romance and Reality of AIDS Altruism in Africa*, Princeton, NJ, and Oxford, UK: Princeton University Press.

Teets, J. C. (2014) *Civil Society Under Authoritarianism: The China Model*, New York, NY: Cambridge University Press.

Terriquez, V. (2011) Schools for Democracy: Labor Union Participation and

References

Latino Immigrant Parents' School-Based Civic Engagement. *American Sociological Review*, 76: 581–601.

Theiss-Morse, E. & Hibbing, J. R. (2005) Citizenship and Civic Engagement. *Annual Review of Political Science*, 8: 227–50.

Tocqueville, A. D. ([1840] 2004) *Democracy in America*, New York, NY: Library of America.

Tsutsui, K. (2017) Human Rights and Minority Activism in Japan: Transformation of Movement Actorhood and Local–Global Feedback Loop. *American Journal of Sociology*, 122: 1050–103.

Tuğal, C. (2017) *Caring for the Poor: Islamic and Christian Benevolence in a Liberal World*, New York, NY, and Abingdon, UK: Routledge.

Unger, J. (ed.) (2008) *Associations and the Chinese state: Contested Spaces*, Armonk, NY: M. E. Sharpe.

United Nations Human Rights Council (2021) *COVID-19: The Road to Recovery and the Essential Role of Civil Society* [Online]. Available: https://undocs.org/pdf?symbol=en/A/HRC/47/L.1.

Verba, S., Schlozman, K. L., & Brady, H. E. (1995) *Voice and Equality: Civic Voluntarism in American Politics*, Cambridge, MA, and London, UK: Harvard University Press.

Walder, A. G. & Gong, X. (1993) Workers in the Tiananmen Protests: The Politics of the Beijing Workers' Autonomous Federation. *The Australian Journal of Chinese Affairs* 29: 1–29.

Wallerstein, I. (2004) *World-Systems Analysis: An Introduction*, Durham, NC, and London, UK: Duke University Press.

Walsh, K. C. (2004) *Talking About Politics: Informal Groups and Social Identity in American Life*, Chicago, IL, and London, UK: University of Chicago Press.

Walsh, K. C. (2007) *Talking About Race: Community Dialogues and the Politics of Difference*, Chicago, IL, and London, UK: University of Chicago Press.

Warner, M. (2002) Publics and Counterpublics. *Public Culture*, 14: 49–90.

Wedeen, L. (2008) *Peripheral Visions: Publics, Power, and Performance in Yemen*, Chicago, IL: University of Chicago Press.

Whittier, J. G. (1839) The Poetical Works in Four Volumes, Boston, New York: Houghton Mifflin and Co., 1892; Bartleby.com, 2013.

Wickham, C. R. (2015) *The Muslim Brotherhood: Evolution of an Islamist Movement*, Princeton, NJ, and Oxford, UK: Princeton University Press.

Wilson, J. (2000) Volunteering. *Annual Review of Sociology*, 26: 215–40.

Wilson, J. & Musick, M. (1997) Who Cares? Toward an Integrated Theory of Volunteer Work. *American Sociological Review*, 62: 694–713.

Wollebaek, D. & Selle, P. (2002) Does Participation in Voluntary Associations Contribute to Social Capital? The Impact of Intensity, Scope, and Type. *Nonprofit and Voluntary Sector Quarterly*, 31: 32–61.

Wu, F. (2017) An Emerging Group Name "Gongyi": Ideational Collectivity in China's Civil Society. *China Review*, 17: 123–50.

References

Wu, W. (2014) Subtle Influences of the Polish "Solidarność." *New York Times (Chinese version)*, February 9.

Wuthnow, R. (1987) *Meaning and Moral Order: Explorations in Cultural Analysis*, Berkeley, CA: University of California Press.

Wuthnow, R. (1991) *Acts of Compassion: Caring for Others and Helping Ourselves*, Princeton, NJ: Princeton University Press.

Xinhua News Agency. (2019) *Xi Jinping Meets Delegates to the 11th National Meeting of the Red Cross Society of China; Li Keqiang, Wang Huning, and Wang Qishan Join the Meeting* [Online]. Available: https://www.redcross.org.cn/html/2019-09/62086_1.html.

Xu, B. (2017) *The Politics of Compassion: The Sichuan Earthquake and Civic Engagement in China*, Stanford, CA: Stanford University Press.

Xu, Y. & Ngai, N.-P. (2011) Moral Resources and Political Capital: Theorizing the Relationship Between Voluntary Service Organizations and the Development of Civil Society in China. *Nonprofit and Voluntary Sector Quarterly*, 40: 247–69.

Yabanci, B. (2019) Turkey's Tamed Civil Society: Containment and Appropriation Under a Competitive Authoritarian Regime. *Journal of Civil Society*, 15: 285–306.

Yanacopulos, H. (2016) *International NGO Engagement, Advocacy, Activism: The Faces and Spaces of Change*, London, UK: Palgrave Macmillan.

Yukich, G., Fulton, B. R., & Wood, R. L. (2019) Representative Group Styles: How Ally Immigrant Rights Organizations Promote Immigrant Involvement. *Social Problems*, 67: 488–506.

Zanotti, L. (2010) Cacophonies of Aid, Failed State Building and NGOs in Haiti: Setting the Stage for Disaster, Envisioning the Future. *Third World Quarterly*, 31: 755–71.

Zhan, Y. (2020) The Moralization of Philanthropy in China: NGOs, Voluntarism, and the Reconfiguration of Social Responsibility. *China Information*, 34: 68–87.

Index

Index

Index

Index

consolidation of 7, 9, 76, 128, 129–30
constructionist theory 9, 51
defining 9
deliberative 20, 28–9, 104, 105
democratic social life 9, 10, 11, 112, 117, 119, 126
discursive theory 9
participatory liberal theory 9, 51
"popular democracy" 25
representative democracy 112, 124, 126
school of democracy thesis 103, 108, 109, 120, 121–2, 135
social democracy 118
stealth democracy 112, 113
Third Wave Democracy 10, 29
unitary democracy 33–4
democratic conversations *see* formal deliberation; rational discourse
democratic imagination 83
democratic social life 9, 10, 11, 112, 117, 119, 126
development policies and measures 153–4, 160
Dewey, John 9
different views, exposure to 103–4, 105
disinformation 2, 18, 105, 144, 181–2
state-sponsored 176
Dodge, Jennifer 109
dramatic narrative 57–8
Dromi, Shai M. 167
Dubček, Alexander 118
Dunant, Henry 165, 167, 168
Durkheim, Emile 37, 41

East Asian societies and values 48–9
echo chamber effect 105, 106, 107
Egypt 158
Arab Spring 134, 158
civil society 133–5, 157
Eliasoph, Nina 80, 81, 111, 113

emotional discourse 52, 54–5, 56
empowerment programs 161
environmentalism 155
Equal Justice Initiative 5
equality 11, 12, 20, 37, 45, 47, 63, 65, 66, 84, 85, 109, 118, 121, 123, 129, 151, 180
essentialism 152
European Union (EU) 174, 176
Eurozone crisis 175
exclusionary practices and rhetoric 11–12, 26, 44, 45, 64, 72, 74, 85, 147
expressive individualism 7, 81, 93, 94
extremism, online 106, 107

Falun Gong 133
Fan, Yun 48–9, 55
fascism 73–4, 89
Ferree, Myra Marx 51
Fine, Gary Alan 78
Finnemore, Martha 166
"flawed democracy" 116, 129
flying universities 121–2
formal deliberation 19–20, 28–40, 105
gendered 38–40
political-cultural context 30
public deliberation programs 30–1
solidarity–adversary tension 33, 35
storytelling 31–3
styles and norms of discourse 31–40
France 116
Frank, David J. 155
Frankfurt School 182
Fraser, Nancy 22, 26, 55, 173
fraternity/ies 69, 72, 74
see also associational life; solidarity
freedom of speech 21, 104
Freud, Sigmund 167
Fulton, Brad R. 79

Index

Index

Index